Land Rover
Discovery

First published in 2002 as *You & Your Land Rover Discovery*
This edition published in January 2009

British Library cataloguing-in-publication data:
A catalogue record for this book is available from the British Library

ISBN 978 184425 557 3

Library of Congress catalog card no. 2008933797

Published by Haynes Publishing, Sparkford, Yeovil, Somerset BA22 7JJ, UK

Tel: 01963 442030 Fax: 01963 440001
Int. tel: +44 1963 442030 Int. fax: +44 1963 440001
E-mail: sales@haynes-manuals.co.uk
Website: www.haynes.co.uk

Haynes North America, Inc.,
861 Lawrence Drive, Newbury Park, California 91320, USA

Printed and bound in Great Britain by J. H. Haynes & Co. Ltd,
Sparkford, Yeovil, Somerset BA22 7JJ

ACKNOWLEDGEMENTS

Thanks, of course, to everyone involved in the production of this book, notably
the following individuals/companies who were pivotal in supplying equipment,
information, and photographs or photographic opportunities: Clifford Electronics,
Eberspächer pre-heaters (John Jennings), Goodyear Great Britain Limited (Ron
Pike), Iwema Enterprise (Hugo Van Osch, Chris Crane and Gordon Finlay),
Landcraft off-road centre (David Mitchell and Dylan Williams for off-road
photography), LEGS (Land Rover Engines & Gearboxes) (Alan Chambers), MAD
Suspension (Clive Berry and Wim Nells), McDonalds Landrover Limited (Rupert
Astbury and Andy McDonald), Paddock Spares, Pharmhouse Marketing (Mark
Adams, ECU specialist), RPi Engineering (Chris Crane and 'Holly' Hollingdale, for
everything V8), and Scorpion Racing 4x4 Centre (Colin Aldred).

Unless credited otherwise, all the pictures in this book are either my own or the
property of Land Rover Limited, to whom many thanks.

Dave Pollard
November 2008

Haynes Enthusiast Guide

Land Rover
Discovery

LAND ROVER

BX02 YFJ

LAND ROVER DISCOVERY
CONTENTS

INTRODUCTION
DISCOVER...

Automotive 'legends' are thick on the ground nowadays; almost anything in production for more than five years gets the tag, and 'classics' often start at 10 years. Land Rover, however has more experience than most at producing these (albeit often more by lucky happenstance than design) and all are legends of true substance rather than the ad-man's spin. The daddy of them all, the eponymous Defender, is still in production – and still recognisable – after 60 years of continuous production. To produce a genuine classic of this stature is impressive enough, but in 1970 the Range Rover repeated the trick. The original (actually latterly named the 'Classic') was produced for 26 years and it is currently riding high in its third generation heading rapidly for the four-decade marker with that 60-year target in its sights. And in 1989, Land Rover performed a hat trick, by launching the Discovery. Like the Range Rover, it too followed the basic Land Rover principle of putting a largely aluminium body on a hefty steel chassis and equipping it with go-anywhere underpinnings. Like its big brother, it's now in its third incarnation, though the S3 is very 21st century and in technological terms, a world away from the first models.

In a Discovery, you get an awful lot for your money; a diesel will give reasonable economy, and if your pockets are deep enough, there's nothing quite like being whooshed along by eight-cylinders of petrol-powered majesty. It can carry 5–7 people and/or lots of luggage, it's a great motorway cruiser and whether on long distance work or trundling around the back-lanes, you'll always be glad of the high-up driving position which allows you to see what's happening miles ahead. Its weight and torque make it a great towing vehicle and, of course, when the going gets rough the Disco gets tough; the four-wheel drive transmission comes into its own, whether the clunky mechanicals of the early 10-speed gearbox (5 high ratios, 5 low ratios) and centre differential lock, or the space-age electronics of the S3, it's virtually impossible for the practised driver to get stuck whatever the conditions. It has managed to create its own niche, carved neatly between the Range Rover, with its upmarket, opulent image, and the Land Rover Defender, the archetypal workhorse. From the start up to the present day, the Discovery has been an award-winner, regularly cleaning-up trophies (Best Tow Car, Best Large Off-Roader etc.) despite serious entries from the opposition. Certainly for the first two incarnations, there's hundreds of companies offering aftermarket products from oil filters to complete engines and most are trying to do so in a way that will please your wallet. (The S3, with its even more complex electronics doesn't lend itself so readily to DIY tinkering, though many owners enjoy adding accessories.)

As if those eminently practical and sensible reasons weren't enough, there's no doubt that the Discovery is a stylish motor to be seen in.

Dave Pollard
November 2008

CHAPTER 1
UNLIKELY BEGINNINGS – DISCOVERY PREHISTORY

Land Rover: the car

The Discovery and Land Rover stories are inextricably linked and the story starts just after the Second World War. In terms of manufacturing production, this period was particularly difficult, not least since steel production was very limited. In order to encourage export, the government offered incentives in the form of extra steel allowance for those who used up some of the aluminium surplus. The managing director of Rover at that time was Spencer Wilks, and whilst he wrestled with this seemingly insoluble problem his brother Maurice had problems of his own. He had a 250-acre farm on the island of Anglesey and there was only one vehicle capable of getting him around the varied terrain – a wartime Willys General Purpose vehicle (shortened to GP and thence to Jeep). As it neared the end of its useful life, Maurice had to consider its replacement; he had almost come to the conclusion that another Jeep was the only answer when it dawned on him that this huge gap in the market could be manna from heaven for Rover.

Both Maurice and Spencer saw immediately the potential in building a 'British Jeep' and started working on the project straight away. At a board meeting in 1947, they were able to show a working prototype. They told the board that the Land Rover (the name had already been decided) would use a Rover P3 engine, gearbox, and rear axle, and that there would be no need for expensive body dies – the entire body would be made from aluminium.

Built in the summer of 1947, all the early prototypes had a tractor-like, centrally-mounted steering wheel. This unusual arrangement was intended to save time and money by avoiding the need to build separate right-hand drive and left-hand drive models for different export markets. By the time the Land Rover was in production the idea had been dropped, but rumours that one of the prototypes still exists somewhere crop up again and again.

The basic guidelines used in the Land Rover's development leaned heavily on its usefulness to the farming community; it had to go anywhere a tractor could and have a power take-off to enable it to use existing farm machinery. A range of bolt-on accessories would further enhance its appeal. The same thinking was also applied when considering export sales, and the car was put forward as the vehicle to tackle everything from harsh deserts to dense jungles and, well, just about everything in-between.

First showing

It was only one year after the concept was first aired that the Land Rover was shown to the public. It featured the 1,595cc engine as used in the Rover P3, which produced 50bhp. Its 80-inch wheelbase was exactly the same as the Willys Jeep, and other similarities included the separate box section chassis frame, and front-mounted engine/gearbox with transfer box at the rear driving propeller shafts to the front and rear live axles. Suspension comprised telescopic dampers and semi-elliptic (cart) springs. Because of cost restrictions, the chassis sections were made from four strips of sheet steel welded together to make the 'boxes'. To save the cost of expensive tooling-up, aluminium body panels were used.

The press and public alike were ecstatic, and so began a story of British off-road, four-wheel drive vehicles that has continued for over 60 years and shows no sign of slowing down. The original production run was to have been 1,000 units per year – a figure restricted by the government. After arguing that the Land Rover could have a successful future as an export vehicle, the production was increased. In fact, in the first year of production, a staggering 8,000 Land Rovers were produced.

← Probably the most famous Land Rover in the world, and certainly the oldest survivor, this is 'Huey' (registration HUE 166), the first pre-production Series 1 (chassis number R01).

↑ Yes, truly, this car is a direct ancestor of the Discovery sitting on your driveway. And what's more, there are far more direct links than seem credible, not least the ladder chassis and Birmabright bodywork. It's actually an 80-inch Series 1. (Nick Dimbleby)

→ Move forward in time around 30 years and you find this Series 3 model. It's hard to see many obvious changes – the headlamps have moved and the wheelbase has gained a couple of inches, but essentially it's still the same car.

The series cars

Over the years Land Rover has consistently changed its specification, occasionally launching 'new' models, but never straying far from the original 'go-anywhere, do-anything' concept that was so right in 1948. The engine size was gradually increased, petrol and diesel options were offered, and both six-cylinder and V8 options were available at various times. The wheelbase grew steadily longer and seating arrangements varied from two people plus load to the equivalent of a small coach party! But right up to its demise in 1985, the Land Rover was always recognisable as such; moreover, the very last car off the production line was clearly a close relative of the first model to hit the streets.

Wheelbase (inches)		Produced from:	To:
Series I	80	1948	1954
	86	1954	1956
	88	1957	1958
	107	1955	1958
	109	1957	1958
Series II	88	1958	1961
	109	1962	1971
Series IIA	88	1962	1971
	109	1962	1971
Series III	88	1972	1984
	109	1972	1984
	109 V8	1979	1985

Onward and upward: the Range Rover

For over 20 years Land Rover's products were gradually improved, with nips and tucks being applied at regular intervals. But whereas a time-traveller from 1950 would find few surprises on any Land Rover vehicle made in 1969, he would have found the great innovation of the following year quite eye-catching. The Range Rover wasn't so much evolution as outright revolution. All of a sudden, four-wheel drive wasn't limited to sluggish, basic Land Rovers driven by farmers carrying three sheep and a bale of hay.

In one fell swoop, the company changed the face of the 4x4 market forever, inventing a new category of off-roader for those who don't really need one and/or want a vehicle that performs on-road as well. Though essentially the same as the traditional Land Rover – large chassis, Birmabright body panels, four-wheel

drive, high and low ratio gearbox, etc – it was a chalk and cheese comparison. The fitment of conventional coil springs and dampers (rather than the archaic leaf springs of its forebears) massively improved the vehicle's road manners and passenger comfort, whilst at the same time increasing axle articulation off-road. What's more, it started to acquire a certain upmarket cachet, and before Land Rover knew what was happening eager buyers were queuing round the block and down the next street. This despite the fact that there was no automatic option, no diesel engine available, and a choice of three doors or go without.

Trying to evolve the Range Rover in the conventional manner was made more difficult by the UK car industry's problems at the time. Money was

↑ **The Range Rover proved to be a huge sales success, incredibly competent on- and off-road and a style icon to boot (it's been exhibited in the Louvre museum in Paris as a work of automotive art). During its 26 year span, it changed from a semi-working tool for the rich farmer to a luxury carriage for those, literally, wanting to rise above the herd. (Nick Dimbleby)**

DID YOU KNOW?

Within months of production starting, Land Rovers were being entered into production 'trials' – off-road competitions similar to motorcycle trials, where the object was to get through difficult off-road stages unaided. It wasn't long before separate 4x4 competitions had to be held, such was the Land Rovers' domination over two-wheel drive entrants. These trials are still very popular today, with various classes being available and many 1950s vehicles entering.

↑ **With the Series 2 car, the luxury theme was taken still further, though the basic styling cues which made its predecessor so famous and successful were wisely retained. This is a 2.5 DSE model.**

tight – or on occasion non-existent – and for many years it appeared that the result of so many hands pulling at the corporate wheel was that the ship just went round in circles. This was extremely annoying for the boys at Land Rover, because the Range Rover was enormously popular, having opened up a niche for comfortable off-roaders that were equally at home on the tarmac or axle-deep in mud. The opposition wasn't hamstrung in the same way and the Japanese in particular soon had plenty of options on the market for buyers who couldn't afford the Range Rover or couldn't be doing with the waiting list (which lasted for many years). Or perhaps they wanted an automatic gearbox, something not available on the Range Rover until 1982 (and even then it was the rather dated and clunky Chrysler Torqueflite three-speed unit). And many owners just couldn't live with

the V8's fuel thirst and needed diesel power, which didn't materialise until 1986 – 16 years after the Range Rover's introduction! As the 1980s drew to a close, Land Rover did manage to get into its stride, making the most of its upmarket image, pushing its equipment levels and price well into the stratosphere. The basic carburetted V8 became fuel injected and grew from 3.5 litres to 3.9 and eventually 4.2. The unimpressive, Italian VM diesel was replaced by Land Rover's own 200 Tdi unit and the car gained the four-speed ZF auto 'box, much to everyone's delight.

By the time the 'new' Range Rover appeared in 1994, the vehicle wasn't so much seen as an upmarket Land Rover, to be used as a working tool as well as a normal car, but more as an alternative to a Jaguar or Mercedes. For two years, the original vehicle – which had become the Classic – was produced alongside the new model, but production finally ended in 1996.

The Series 2 Range Rover was an evolution of its illustrious ancestor, retaining all the styling cues which immediately identified it – notably the fluted, clamshell bonnet and horizontally split rear tailgate. It, too, was built on a separate chassis and was constructed largely of Birmabright panels over a steel underbody. Inside,

DID YOU KNOW?
If you fancy an early Land Rover but can't face the hassle of restoration or the price of a finished car, there's a way to scale down the cost by scaling down the vehicle; as well as running his off-roading site in Wales, David Mitchell has the world's largest stock of Land Rover models.

← The monocoque body/chassis marked a real move away from tradition.

↓ In the millennium year, Land Rover celebrated 30 years of the Range Rover. From front to rear we see: a Series 2 30th anniversary LE special edition, a long wheel-base LSE model, the first ever Range Rover Series 1, and the last Range Rover 'Classic'.

↑ Not quite the sort
of interior you'd hose
out after a long day on
the farm! This 2001
Autobiography has just
about everything you
can think of, including
satellite navigation.

← The Series 3 Range
Rover was bigger,
more powerful, more
electronically complex
– in fact, it was just plain
more. It still retained
the classic Range Rover
features, notably that
fluted bonnet and …

↑ ... horizontally split rear tailgate.
It might look as if it was a variation on
the 1970 theme ...

↓ ... and it could still cut it off-road –
if you were prepared to treat your £65,000
investment this way.

there was absolutely no pretension at being a working
vehicle – unless your work took you stockbroking.
There were buttons to press, levers to pull, and most
models came swathed in leather.

Whereas the Series 1 Range Rover stayed in
production over 25 years, its successor managed just
eight years before giving way to the startling Series 3
model. Production of the Series 3 began in December
2001 and it was available from March 2002 (postponed
a month from its original, ambitious 15 February launch
date). It retained the famous bonnet flutes and split
rear tailgate, but as for virtually every other aspect, it
was as different as you could get. For the first time, a
monocoque body with integrated chassis was used, the
vehicle was around half a ton heavier than previously,
and its exterior dimensions showed that it was clearly
designed with America in mind, where the roads are
wide enough for a car of this size – the rustic back lanes
of Devon or Derbyshire are not the Series 3's home
territory. But despite its seriously upmarket intentions,
it still had all the off-road prowess one would expect,
with full-time four-wheel drive and a boatload of
electronic devices to stop slipping and sliding and to
keep the car going when the going got tough.

← Back in the Tardis again, to find a Land Rover Defender 90 (originally just called the 90), this being the County Station Wagon model. It's a bit chunkier, a bit longer and there's a really modern(!) one-piece windscreen, but there's no doubting its lineage from the model on page 10. If you need convincing of the Land Rover link, check out those standard-issue Discovery alloy wheels, as fitted to most other cars in the range at the time.

→ The Land Rover 110 was introduced a year ahead of the 90 in 1984 (it too became a Defender), and though it doesn't quite have the cachet of its shorter sibling, it's massively popular for its practical benefits. As ever, it's available in a zillion different packages, this particular one being the station wagon with enough seats for the whole street.

Refining the Land Rover: the 90, 110, and Defender

However, there was still a huge market for those who actually needed a tough four-wheel drive machine and it was clear that as the 1970s came to a close, the Land Rover stranglehold on the market had weakened considerably. Competition, particularly from Japanese companies such as Mitsubishi, Toyota, and Daihatsu, was fierce; the products were tough, reliable and, more importantly, modern and comfortable. No longer was it necessary for a working vehicle to be hard work in itself.

So in 1983 Land Rover chose the Geneva Motor Show for the launch of the replacement for its eponymous go-anywhere 4x4; and not without some serious trepidation. They faced the problem of bringing what was essentially a 30-year-old design right up to date, but in a way that didn't alienate its existing clientele. First off the blocks was the 110 model, which followed the tradition of naming models after the (approximate) wheelbase length, in inches of course – no millimetres here (the Land Rover 2794 wouldn't have quite the same ring to it!).

To a great extent, the 110 and the 90 were essentially re-bodied Range Rovers. Look underneath and you'll see a remarkably similar ladder chassis, damper/spring arrangement, and gearbox/engine combination, etc. Compared to the S3 Land Rover, the 110 had a higher, single-piece windscreen, wider track, more comfortable seats, wind-up windows, modern interior trim, 'trendy' wheel arch extensions, and even an air conditioning option. But even from across the street, it was from all angles unmistakably a Land Rover and was immediately accepted. The first engine line-up was a choice of the familiar 2.25 petrol and diesel engines, though the diesel became 2.5 litres in 1985 and was turbocharged the following year to help it keep up with the opposition. The

ubiquitous V8 engine was also available. The four-cylinder cars were fitted with a five-speed gearbox.

In 1984 the three-door version, the 90, arrived on the scene and proved to be even more popular, especially with hardened off-roaders, who relished the lack of overhang at either end which enabled them to drive to areas previously the sole preserve of mountain goats. A real treat was the introduction in 1985 of the V8 option in the 90 – as long as you had shares in BP.

In September 1990, the 90 and 110 models both became 'Defenders', with minor modifications here and there, and a major engine-bay improvement with the installation of the 200 Tdi diesel engine, a great improvement on the increasingly outdated units fitted since its launch. In 1994 the Defenders kept in line with other Land Rover products as the 200 Tdi unit was phased out to make way for the 300 Tdi. At the same time, the tougher R380 manual five-speed gearbox was fitted.

Land Rover were not only happy to have replaced what seemed irreplaceable, but also that they had done so using parts-bin technology. The new models were consequently not only successful but were relatively cheap to produce. As we shall see in the next chapter, this approach would later prove itself again, with another Land Rover vehicle. Guess which one …?

↑ **In 1999 Land Rover launched the limited edition Defender Heritage. In contrast to the retro-look front grille, the interior featured full leather trim, a milled-aluminium gear knob and air conditioning – a far cry from its spartan Mk I ancestors.**

CHAPTER 2
A STAR IS BORN

Achieving the impossible

Coming up with a new car, from sitting at the drawing board to pulling the covers off it at a motor show, is a long process. Developing exterior profiles, interior designs, engine specifications and outputs, marketing considerations and, of course, coming up with the hard cash, all mean that it is a process that just can't be hurried. Thing is, no one told Land Rover, because from its conception in 1986 it was just two-and-a-half years before the wraps were removed and the Discovery was shown to an impressed motoring public.

Project Jay

Range Rover can be credited with having opened up a new market in the UK – one for 4x4 off-road machines which could quite happily be used every day of the week. As the 1980s progressed this market began to burgeon and diversify into various sectors. Suzuki carved a neat little niche for itself with a derivation of the small LJ series, the Vitara. Though often maligned, this was extremely capable off-road and, more importantly, managed to make the small 4x4 market very lucrative. Toyota's RAV4 followed and then Land Rover, too, got involved, with the highly successful Freelander. At the other end of the scale Toyota, Mitsubishi, and Nissan were all having a crack at the Range Rover; and in between, there was a growing market for mid-range, 'lifestyle' off-roaders.

It was here that Land Rover had no representative and was losing out to its Japanese rivals, who had stolen a march. Under the guidance of MD Tony Gilroy, a team (called the Swift group) was formed to see how best to right this particular wrong. The new vehicle, whatever it might be, was code-named Project Jay.

The first problem the team came up against was the fact that many cars came in either short or long wheelbase models, something prohibitively expensive for the British company to handle. How about, they pondered, a single vehicle that straddled the two wheelbases; something longer than the Defender 90 but shorter than the 110? Einstein wasn't required to work out that the Range Rover's 100-inch chassis fitted the bill nicely. By using existing Range Rover underpinnings (axles, drivetrain, and suspension) etc, the company saved an awful lot of time and not a little cash. One major difference when looking under the car was that the Boge self-levelling suspension was not fitted to the Discovery. It added complexity and cost and the engineers thought it simpler just to beef up the rear springs to compensate. Anyone who's ever had to purchase a replacement Boge unit will agree with their thinking on this point.

However, being Range Rover-based brought its own problems, because the new vehicle had to be pitched into a totally different market to the older car and be seen as nothing like its bigger brother. It succeeded so well that most owners don't realise that the Series 1 Discovery is in fact longer, taller, and heavier than the car on which it is based. The roof height at the rear was made necessary by the need to provide plenty of headroom for passengers in the 'boot', sitting on the pull-down side seats. The stepped rear roof line could have been just another Daihatsu copy (the Fourtrak already had this feature), but Land Rover made it individual by including a roof light at either side. Apart from looking good from the outside, it also had the effect of making the cabin feel particularly spacious and airy. Because it was now higher than the Range Rover, it was decided to try an optical illusion – cutting off the rear of the car sharply

← **A Discovery proves that it can boldly go where conventional cars fear to tread. (Nick Dimbleby)**

> **DID YOU KNOW?**
> Unlike the original Range Rover, the Discovery was always designed to be both a three-door and a five-door vehicle. Check out the size of the front doors on either model – they're the same.

(compare it with the Range Rover's angled back) not only disguised the height but made the Discovery look shorter, too. The extra height meant that the roof had to be steel in order to give extra structural strength to the taller car, the Range Rover roof being aluminium. The company also raided the parts bin for things like door handles (Morris Marina), headlamps (Sherpa van), and tail lamps (Maestro van).

Inside, there was plenty of competition among designers, but it was 1980s style gurus, Conran Design, that won out in the end, though Land Rover's own design team did have some input. The need to attract the young, 'lifestyle' customer with a bright and airy interior was the prime consideration, as was getting away from the more 'serious' interior of the Range Rover. As with most things based on trends, the interior can look a bit dated to modern eyes, but even so, it's still functional in a way that many older cars could never hope to be, with most switchgear and controls being in just the right place. The biggest real hassle was the siting of the radio/cassette deck, the position of which had to be the same as in the Range Rover; being so low down in the centre console is not at all good for road safety. Moreover, there was precious little room behind the DIN aperture for those who wanted to upgrade to something a little more adventurous.

Discovery milestones

This is a potted history of the Discovery and covers the salient points of its development. By definition and with any car, there are so many tiny changes, options, and upgrades that to deal with the subject in detail would fill a book in itself. I have therefore limited myself to major milestones in the development of Land Rover's most successful single model to date.

The Discovery was launched on 12 September 1989 at the Frankfurt Motor Show and was on general sale from 16 November of that year. It was available with a limited specification; a choice of 200Tdi diesel or 3.5-litre V8 petrol engine, steel wheels, five-speed manual gearbox, and three-door bodyshell. Inside, just about everything was Sonar Blue, fashionable then but rather more questionable in retrospect. However, the overall interior effect was one of space and light, with huge side and rear windows and rear roof lights. This capacious, airy

↑ **This front view of a 1990 V8 model shows a stylish, purposeful design which still stands up today. Most importantly, it didn't look like a Range Rover. It has the optional twin roof rails (with crossbars stowed in a special bag, under the rear seat) and driving lamps. Those soft and vulnerable aluminium flanks had to stay unprotected until the 1992 model year, when five-door models got rubber protective side rubbing strips as standard.**

→ **Let there by light – and there was. It simply flooded into the car via the large glass area and the innovative trademark roof-lights at the rear. Many cars also had twin sunroofs, which gave the cabin an even more airy feel.**

↑ The chunky rear end was necessitated to make the vehicle look smaller than the Range Rover, but actually makes it look good in the process. Unlike its older brother, the rear door is a single-piece unit, hinged on the right.

→ Inside there was a choice of any colour you liked – as long as it was Sonar Blue. Blue seats, blue plastic trim, blue carpet – it was trendy at the time, but could get a bit wearing. Despite this, the dash was very attractive, with clean, modern lines, and easy-to-read and functional dials, and was ergonomically very good.

↑ Only three-door models were available for the first year, though the Discovery was designed to be a five-door car from the beginning, so the front doors on all models were the same size. The trim was attractive, if brittle, and the speakers were standard.

→ Whilst the standard Discovery front seats were reasonable enough, it was generally agreed that they couldn't match up to those of the Range Rover. The answer for many was to do a swap. It's possible to do this quite easily, though the 200 Series cars (pre-facelift) will need special adaptor brackets; on later models it's a straight swap. (Courtesy Nationwide Trim)

↑ Having only three doors meant rear-seat passengers had to struggle for access, especially given the ground clearance of the car. The introduction of the five-door came not a minute too soon for those with families.

feeling was increased still further because most owners took the twin-sunroof option.

In marketing terms, it was important for the new vehicle to be seen as being totally different from the Range Rover, despite its many obvious connections (it was essentially a Range Rover kit car, using its chassis and underpinnings, etc). As such, it was initially only available as a three-door – this implied a young lifestyle, without the encumbrance of children requiring rear doors. It also helped the company's cash-flow by enabling them to spread the cost of tooling-up for the five-door version. Another way of placing the Discovery below the Range Rover was to make the only petrol option the carburettor-fed V8 engine, rather than the fuel-injected unit. The garish stripes down the flanks of the car were another attempt to appeal to a trendy younger clientele.

The price was certainly eye-catching, at less than £16,000, but once again the marketing boys had been at work. Buying a Discovery at the basic price would leave you with a very low-rent Discovery indeed; electric windows, central locking, sunroofs, front mud flaps, and even a rear parcel shelf, were all there, but only on the list of optional extras. Air conditioning was an option only on the petrol-

engined Discoverys. Another extra, destined to become an archetypal Discovery feature, was that of twin, inward-facing rear seats. These effectively removed all the luggage space when in use, but meant that the car became a seven-seater. They folded neatly into the side when not in use. Whilst most adults would baulk at spending too long in the tiny seats, children loved them, a real factor in the Discovery's soon to be adopted role of school-run-favourite. The trademark stepped section at the rear of the roof was there largely to allow the necessary rear seat headroom – remember that the seats are located directly above the fuel tank. Up top, the roof rails, with quickly-detachable cross-bars, were made an option, though few cars left the factory without them. Given fuel prices at the time, it was no real surprise to find that diesel sales outstripped the V8-powered cars by over three to one.

In 1990, Land Rover bosses entered the new decade on a high, as sales for the first six months of the year made their new baby the best-selling car in its class, with showrooms shifting almost twice the total of its nearest rival. They celebrated at the UK Motor Show by launching the five-door model, something the public had been demanding since the

↙ ↓ **Most Discoverys left the factory with twin, inward-facing seats in this position (the belts would normally be stored behind the seat back). When not in use they folded away neatly as here, and it was the work of seconds to pull them down into position. Lap belts were provided for both. Having the seats thus was a brilliant stroke of marketing, particularly as having all that extra light in the rear, together with the height provided by the stepped rear roof section, made it a pleasant place to be – as long as you weren't too tall; adults seldom find it much fun in there!**

car's introduction. Whereas the three-door model had been aimed at the youth market, the five-door was aimed squarely at the younger family drivers, those motorists with responsibilities but without the need for fripperies such as side stripes (which were binned anyway). These eminently sensible folk were pampered with standard-fit central locking, headlamp washers, electric windows, electric door mirrors, inward-facing rear seats, roof rails, luggage roller blind, and attractive five-spoke alloy wheels.

Inside, those sated with a surfeit of Sonar could opt for Bahama Beige – hardly the choice of champions, but possibly a little less wearing on the senses over time. In the load area, owners were very pleased to find that the anchorages for the three seat belts (two inertia reel and one lap belt) had been made flush with the floor (previously they had protruded more than an inch, which had made carrying long/flat loads very difficult with the rear seats folded). Diesel owners had let the company know that they were fed up with constantly playing with the heating controls, so air conditioning was made available as an option on all models rather than just the V8.

The minority that preferred (and could afford!) the thirst of the V8 petrol engine were pleased to

note that the ex-Range Rover 3.5-litre EFi engine was available in place of the relatively sluggish and even more thirsty twin-carb version. Power was up, to 163bhp (153bhp when supplied with the optional catalyst), and torque too, to a useful 212lb ft (287Nm).

Sales continued to keep the bosses happy, with the five-door in particular proving very popular. It's hardly off-the-wall conjecture to speculate that they were being bought largely by younger couples with small children who still needed lots of practicality and space but who wanted to drive something different and stylish. When faced with the choice of a Volvo estate or the Discovery, there didn't seem much competition. And you can't imply you've spent the weekend troubling the upper reaches of Ben Nevis in a conventional two-wheel drive saloon!

Gearbox troubles had afflicted many of the early cars, and to try and address this the LT77 'box was given uprated first and second gear synchromesh for 1991 and renamed the LT77S. By and large, this addressed the irritating problem of getting second gear when the unit was cold, when it could be very recalcitrant to engage. From the outside, the 1992 spec five-door models could be identified by the

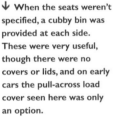

↓ **When the seats weren't specified, a cubby bin was provided at each side. These were very useful, though there were no covers or lids, and on early cars the pull-across load cover seen here was only an option.**

↑ The luggage area was plenty large enough for most items, and if required the split rear seats could be folded forward to give even more space. Note the protruding first-year style seat-belt anchorages, which were a nuisance when trying to load flat items with the rear seats folded forwards. On the back of the right-hand seat can be seen the zip-up cover for the removable sunroof. Note the black brackets at each side of the vehicle, part of the official Land Rover dog guard accessory kit.

↖ The roller-blind style rear load cover is definitely worth seeking out in order to keep nefarious eyes from checking out the valuables in the boot. It fastens over hooks at the rear of the car and the material often snaps with repeated use.

← An interesting option, and one seldom seen nowadays, was the cubby bag, which fitted on the rear of the centre console and took the place of the conventional flip-lid plastic version. The benefit here was that the bag could easily be removed for carrying around. Of course, that was its downfall, as many were taken away and never replaced.

driver and passengers alike. Already, the aftermarket companies had started producing kits for those keen to avoid the 'ship-in-a-gale' feeling when negotiating even the gentlest bend. Inside the car, the effects of the massive rise in car-crime were apparent in the fitment as standard of an electronic engine immobiliser/alarm.

Fans of easy-shifting were rewarded when the rather nice ZF 22HP4, four-speed automatic gearbox was introduced, albeit as an extra-cost option and only for the V8-engined models. It had already gained a good reputation for its smooth operation and reliability in the Range Rover. Better still, it meant Discovery owners never had to endure the previous Land Rover automatic, the Borg-Warner Torqueflite three-speed unit, with its distinctly clunky action. However, whilst Range Rover owners luxuriated (still further) with a chain-driven transfer box, Discovery drivers were left with the original gear-driven unit. That said, constant development meant that this was much quieter than in previous seasons, so it wasn't too much hassle.

An unusual introduction in 1993 was the Mpi model. On the surface, fitting a 2-litre engine into the Discovery seems to make little sense, especially when it was designed with 'normal' cars in mind. In this case, the four-cylinder 1,994cc engine originally saw service in the Rover 820i saloon and its smaller, coupé sibling, where its 134bhp endowed them with plenty of performance. But whilst a torque output of 137lb ft (186Nm) would have been equally impressive in those cars, in the two-tonne Discovery it was rather less so. Moreover, the revvy nature of the 16v engine meant that peak torque didn't arrive until 2,500rpm. So why bother? Land Rover had realised that in certain markets there were great benefits to be had by coming in with an engine under 2 litres. For example, in Italy petrol engines over that capacity paid a hefty premium in terms of road fund tax compared with cars of a smaller engine capacity.

Another less than thoroughly successful venture came courtesy of the Honda Motor Company, which at that time had a stake in Rover. They were keen to make some sales in the massive Japanese 4x4 market, but had nothing home-grown to offer. Their answer was to re-badge the V8i Discovery as the Honda Highway, sit back, and wait for the cash to roll in. Unfortunately buyers weren't so keen on a Honda-badged Rover, although sales of the Land Rover-badged product continued apace.

↑ **No surprises in the gearbox department; the car-based, LT77 five-speed gearbox was used (renamed the LT77S after an uprate in 1991) together with the ubiquitous Land Rover LT230T transfer box. The front lever was for manually selecting the lower set of gear ratios and locking the centre differential when driving in particularly slippery conditions, such as deep mud or snow.**

rubber side-rubbing strips fitted to protect the vulnerable alloy door and wing panels.

1993 was something of a transition year, as the model settled into the 'establishment' before the more interesting changes of 1994. In driving terms, there was nothing but improvement when front and rear anti-roll bars were made optional across the range. Until then, the pronounced body roll had been one of the car's most irritating features, to some extent even more so than on the Range Rover because of the younger vehicle's increased height and heavier, steel roof. Whilst there was seldom any real danger of the Discovery actually tipping over, it often felt as if it might, which was discomfiting for

← ↑ The speed with which the original Discovery was produced was incredible, but of course, much of this was made possible by some raiding of the corporate parts bins. As we've already seen, much of the running gear, suspension, and brakes came from the Range Rover, but a little lateral thinking saw them sourcing the door handles from the Morris Marina with the tail lamps from the Maestro van and headlamps from the Sherpa van.

↑ ↑ The best of both worlds? The Discovery Commercial was based around the three-door Tdi model and first appeared as an official Land Rover vehicle in 1993. As a workhorse, it's a real-world alternative to a Defender 90 or 110, because it's so much more civilised to drive, especially over long distances.

In 1993 Land Rover started selling the Discovery Commercial – effectively a Discovery van. Vans are exempt from tax in many parts of the world and almost everywhere are financially more beneficial to own for the business customer. Based around a three-door Tdi Discovery, all the rear side windows were blanked off and the rear seat was removed to make way for a single-piece floor. A protective bulkhead was fitted behind the front seats.

The 1994 model year – from September 1993 – was, in fact, the shortest year around, because the 1995 model year began in March 1994! Anyway, the 1994 spec petrol engine option was the 3.9-litre model, as already fitted for four years to the Range Rover. By this time the law required the standard fitment of a catalyst exhaust, which chewed a little of the power and torque off the 'dirty' engine, officially rated at 180bhp and 230lb ft (312Nm) respectively. The 10bhp increase over the 3.5-litre engine was welcome, but even more so was a whopping 50lb ft (68Nm) of torque, especially as it peaked some 1,600rpm down the rev band. This massively increased its drivability and desirability; if only it did a few more mpg!

Diesel buyers – by far the majority – were able to specify an auto 'box for the first time and, unusually, this was available on the Discovery before the Range Rover; indeed, it was the first time Land Rover had ever offered an automatic diesel of any description. It proved to be a good move as, to date, Land Rover reckon that around a quarter of all diesel sales are specified with the auto 'box option.

Car-theft continued to be a real problem, and to help inhibit 'ringing' and similar nefarious activities the VIN (vehicle identification number) was etched on a plate in the dashboard top, clearly visible through the windscreen. It was also repeated in its original position, on the slam panel in the engine bay, although in that position it was still vulnerable to professional thieves.

Project Romulus: the mid-term facelift

The Discovery had been pitched into the cut and thrust of a very competitive market place, and to stay competitive it was necessary to make constant changes. As well as minor updates there was the need to apply a facelift to the whole car roughly halfway into its expected life span, typically around ten years.

The Discovery was due to be launched in America in April 1994, so it made sense to start with the 'facelifted' version. The uprated Discovery was first shown to the public at the Geneva Motor Show in March 1994. As such, everyone got the 1995 model six months early and though we delighted in the merits of the brand new 300 Tdi engine, this was of no interest to the American market, where cheap fuel meant that it was largely irrelevant. However, a USA-plus-point was that their legislation demanded the fitment of protective side-impact bars, so all models received them regardless. It's interesting to note that the facelift car didn't get an 'official' name, so most people refer to it as the 300 series, even when fitted with a V8 engine.

As ever with Land Rover, every project takes on a code name, and the new Discovery project was known as 'Romulus'. Unlike many code names which

↑ The Discovery has long been a favourite with the police forces across the country, especially for motorway duties. (Nick Dimbleby)

↑ The mid-term facelift
gave the Discovery a
much smoother look
all-round. Reducing the
number of slats in the
grille combined with larger
headlamps/indicators and
a new spoiler gave an
altogether more chunky
and aggressive look to
the front.

had weather connections, this one related to the
legend of Romulus and Remus, the twins who were
raised by wolves, and Project Remus was the code
name for the 'new' Range Rover. The use of these
'twin' code names was not an accident, as many
facets of the two cars were common to both.

Land Rover's marketing folk had been at work
again, considering the placement of the 'new' car. As
the Range Rover was moving further up the price
scale, the Discovery had to follow suit. Though this
would leave a gap below it, it wasn't a problem,
because the smaller Freelander was being lined up to
fill it. The cheapest Discovery was listed at £17,640
and there were various options all the way up to the
ES model at £25,765.

From the outside, the changes were subtle
though immediately obvious – if that isn't a total
contradiction in terms. The front grille/headlamp
arrangement was changed to give the car a more
modern appearance. The ex-Maestro van headlamps
were displaced by much larger units, offering much
improved night-time vision, and this meant that the
indicators alongside also had to be redesigned. The
updated front spoiler could still 'spoil' the fun off-

road but had the advantage of being able to house
optional fog lamps (Range Rover style), unlike
earlier models, where they had to be hung from
the bumper.

The Series 1 cars had one lamp cluster at either
side of the rear door, and these housed all the
rear lamps, the bumper housing just a reflector.
However, on the facelift models this cluster
contained only brake, fog, and reversing lamps,
the side lights and indicators having migrated to
the bumper. Quite why it was thought a good
idea to have the indicators so low down remains a
mystery. In fact, such was the adverse reaction that
the clusters were soon replaced with the originals,
although the bumper-mounted indicators remained
as a sort of belt-and-braces measure. Anti-roll bars
were made standard across the range to cheers
from everyone and ABS anti-lock brakes were
made available as an option (and were standard
fitment on the ES model).

In terms of engines, the 3.9-litre stayed as it was,
whilst the still-struggling Mpi unit was endowed
with slightly more power and torque, though this
did little for its popularity. The 300 Tdi was greeted

with much praise. Though with the same capacity and power and torque figures, it was a very different unit to the 200 Tdi, mostly in the areas of refinement and emissions control (see below for further details).

Sitting in the driving seat of a 300 series car, the driver would instantly be aware of the massive change in the dashboard layout. It was much more modern than its predecessor and airbags were optional for both driver and passenger – a first for an off-roader of this type. These were standard on the top-of-the-range ES model and optional on the others. A new range of interior trim options was available, most aimed at giving the car a more 'grown-up' feel. And when the driver went to change gear, he'd also get a surprise, as the manual gearbox 300 series cars were fitted with the R380 'box, which had a different shift pattern to the older LT77S.

In chassis terms, some attention was paid to reducing noise and vibration; and in safety terms, new 'crush cans' were fitted behind the front bumper over-riders. The aim of these was to absorb the initial energy created in a collision, sacrificing themselves in the hope of avoiding more expensive damage to structural parts of the car.

↑ Little things mean a lot – the 200 series cars had to make do with ex-Range Rover door mirrors, but part of the facelift package were these rather stylish items.

↑ It's not easy to tell the revised car from its predecessor at the rear, but look closely at the bumper and you'll see that the indicators have been moved from the rear pillars. A strange move, as they would clearly be less visible to lines of following traffic.

← Another aspect of the facelift models was the blacked-out section around the windscreen.

↑ The indicators were soon moved back to the original position (though the bumper flashers were retained as a 'belt and braces' measure). As you can see from this shot, the cluster has regained the orange indicator section.

→ One of the most important features for the 300 series Discovery was the fitment of a new dashboard. It looked much more modern – the original had dated surprisingly quickly – and was far more ergonomic, siting the radio nearer the driver's line of sight, for example. Better still, it facilitated the installation of airbags, a welcome first for a large 4x4 vehicle.

The new Discovery was a massive hit, even more so than Land Rover expected, and this placed a great strain on the production lines. Build quality had never been a strong point, and with the increased sales demand now placed on the company it was almost inevitable that it should suffer further. One of the biggest casualties was the R380 gearbox, which gave many owners trouble. The general piecing together of the car was almost slapdash in places and it's a mark of just how good the car was that it continued to chalk up very respectable sales, despite its problems.

During 1996 Electronic Diesel Control (EDC) was introduced on Tdi engines – but only if they were mated to an automatic gearbox. In order to redress the performance balance that a self-shifter inevitably creates, the clever electronics produced some extra power and torque, bringing the totals to 120bhp and 221lb ft (300Nm). Those lucky folk in the USA got a 4.0-litre uprated V8 engine, but the V8 specification stayed the same in the UK.

Having been the best-seller in its class since its inception, the Discovery excelled itself this year by outselling its nearest competitor by a staggering 80 per cent. That said, the actual sales were showing a downward trend as the car started to show its age, despite its recent revamp. More than a few people were looking ahead to the much rumoured (and often spy-shotted) new model and deciding that it might be wise to wait for that.

Despite all the good intentions and financial logic, the Discovery-buying public were not swayed by the Mpi model, and from October 1997 the never-popular 2-litre Discovery was deleted from the catalogues. Again, the many and various model designations were changed round, muddying the waters for then-new buyers and even more so for anyone buying used a few years later. Six colours were added to the specifications list, the most important aspect of which was that they incorporated the ecologically-sound, water-borne technology. The colours were Caledonian Blue, White Gold, Rutland Red, Woodcote Green, Cobar Blue, and Chawton White.

↗ → The 300 Tdi engine looks similar to its forebear, though there are many differences, despite the identical power and torque figures. The most obvious visual difference is the attention to sound-proofing on the top of the unit, which can be seen clearer below. Note the turbo sitting in a similar position to the 200 Tdi unit.

↑ The 1998 Discovery Safari was another special edition – the last of the Series 1 cars, in fact. Again, there were lots of standard extras, not least the front bull-bar, heavily padded following a controversy surrounding the possible safety implications. Prices were £26,995 and £28,575 for the Tdi manual and auto respectively and £28,725 for the V8i auto.

All models were fitted with a high-level rear brake lamp, in order to meet legislation and improve safety, particularly when travelling in close-company on busy motorways. Electric front windows and headlamp levelling became standard fitments across the board and when alloy wheels were fitted, an alloy spare was included rather than a steel wheel, as previously.

In marketing-speak, the price structure continued to be revised upwards – ie there were price rises.

Tdi Commercial three-door	£21,135
Tdi Estate three-door	£20,995
Tdi XS three-door	£22,515
V8i XS three-door	£22,895
Tdi Estate five-door	£22,995
Tdi GS five-door	£24,995
V8i GS five-door	£25,465
Tdi XS five-door	£26,995
V8i XS five-door	£27,465
Tdi ES five-door	£30,750
V8i ES five-door	£31,220

As can be seen from this table, there was a plethora of model designations still available – and this doesn't include any of the special editions.

All talk in 1998 was, not unnaturally, of the Discovery replacement. What would it be called?

Quite wisely, the Land Rover top brass decided to keep the name the same as a matter of course, but before its launch there was plenty of production of the original model still to be sold. The motor industry has long taken the 'special edition' route as a simple way to perk-up sales of an out-going model which might otherwise stick as buyers anticipated something new. The previous year had seen the Goodwood, 500 cars all finished in British Racing Green, with a host of special features including an uprated stereo system, deep dish alloy wheels, and burr walnut interior trim. However, the Goodwood race track took exception to Land Rover using its name and so all but one of the special editions were delivered without the 'Goodwood' badges – and without a replacement to take its place. In June of that year, the five-door Argyll special edition was announced. This time 600 cars were made (with a name that stuck), the buyers getting those deep dish wheels again and having a choice of exterior paintwork (Woodcote Green or Oxford Blue).

Land Rover introduced several more Discovery 'specials' prior to its demise. In April 1998 the Argyll three-door was launched, based on the 1997 five-door Argyll Limited Edition. It featured lots of executive additions including twin sunroofs, roof rails, headlamp wash, heated door mirrors, silver 'Castor' alloy wheels, 235 section tyres, and front mudflaps as standard. Then there was the Aviemore, using as its starting point the GS model. This was available only in British Racing Green, with a limited range of interior trim colours.

Land Rover continued the special edition theme with its launch of the Anniversary 50 in June 1998. Not surprisingly, this was created to celebrate the 50th anniversary of Land Rover. The standard 'extras' list was long – leather seat facings, air conditioning, CD player, seven seats, roof rails, alloy wheels, front fog lamps, driver airbag, burr walnut fascia detailing, leather steering wheel, and rapid windscreen defrost meant that the owner would want for little. This luxurious model was available in diesel or petrol, three- or five-door variants.

The final UK special Discovery was the Safari, 1,100 of which were produced with five-doors and seven seats, and finished in Epsom Green. This model was positively laden with goodies, including Tornado alloy wheels, air conditioning, a soft-style bull bar with fog lamps, heated windscreen et al.

The Tdi diesel engine: a real Gem-ini

It was clear from the start that the Discovery was going to need a decent diesel power plant to ensure that it could keep up with the opposition. The existing turbo diesel as used in the Land Rover 90 and 110 models was itself an uprate (under the code name Project Falcon) of the company's existing diesel engines. Whilst it did the job sufficiently well, it was clearly not going to be refined enough for the new car. During the early 1980s, Land Rover had been working on a diesel development of the existing, all-aluminium V8, code-named Project Iceberg. On paper it made a lot of sense, as it's simpler to modify an existing unit than to start from scratch; and diesel V8s did well in the USA, giving good mpg and massive amounts of torque – the prime requirement for a large off-roader. However, this project was abandoned in 1983, which is a great shame. The 2.4-litre Italian VM engine (Project Beaver) was fitted in the Range Rover between 1986–92. Despite a

↓ A large number of Land Rover vehicles were used by relief agencies during the troubles in Kosovo. This photo, from 1999, shows a fleet of facelifted Discoverys (with 300 Tdi engines) and 110 Defenders supplied by Land Rover, ready for departure.

mid-term uprate it was generally disliked by both the Press and public, and whilst it returned a reasonable mpg figure it was woefully lacking in performance. The Discovery's opposition – the Mitsubishi Shogun et al – used far more accomplished diesel units, which managed a reasonable performance to match the frugality. The answer, in Discovery terms, was to go one step beyond and create a totally new, direct injection diesel engine – Project Gemini, which eventually became the 200 Tdi.

Direct injection had been employed for some time on larger engines used in lorries, but despite its many good points one major downside was the noise – 'diesel knock' – inherent in the system; not a great problem in a 32-tonne truck, but definitely not what you need in a passenger vehicle. The development team worked closely with Lucas/CAV and Bosch to solve this problem, ultimately deciding to use equipment from the German company. By using rising-rate return springs on the injectors, the initial rate of injection was slowed and the rate of rise of combustion pressure controlled. This latter point was vital, as this was the chief cause of the taxi-like clatter. The Land Rover team also worked with the Austrian AVL company to create a combustion chamber design that would enable the new unit to rev higher and compete on equal terms with the formidable Japanese competition.

Turbocharging the engine proved to be relatively easy, given Land Rover's years of experience with the existing line-up, and a Garrett T25 turbo was matched to a suitable intercooler to provide the boost required. (The 'Tdi' nomenclature came from its three main ingredients – Turbocharged, Direct injection, Intercooler.) The completed 200 Tdi engine turned out to be some 20kg (around 44lb) lighter than the original Land Rover turbo diesel, despite being based around the older block. However, just about every other component was new with the exception of the crank, and even that was uprated.

So, the Discovery was the first 4x4 to be equipped with a direct injection diesel engine, but how did it stack up to its 'direct' opposition within the Land Rover empire? The 2.4-litre VM engine produced 1bhp more, but the Tdi clawed this back and more by turning out 12lb ft (16Nm) more torque some 600rpm down the rev range. Perhaps even more relevant was its torque compared to the 3.5-litre V8 petrol engine which produced 3lb ft (4Nm) less and at 2,000rpm, rather than the diesel's 1,800rpm.

↑ ↑ The small but very efficient Garrett T25 Turbocharger fitted neatly on the nearside of the engine bay. It matched the diesel engine well, showing few signs of the dreaded 'turbo lag'.

↑ In the light of modern diesel technology, the 200 Tdi probably doesn't look like much, but it was a ground-breaking unit and a massive leap forward compared with the previous Land Rover turbo diesel engine. Performance was impressive then and is hardly less so now, producing a prodigious amount of torque and much better fuel economy than the ever-thirsty V8.

It was clear to Land Rover that, as ground-breaking as the 200 Tdi engine was, the opposition was steadily moving the goalposts and that by the time of the Romulus 'facelift' launch it would be outdated. Though in technical terms it was spot-on, it lacked refinement compared to many of its rivals and customers were now more demanding – it was no longer necessary for diesel owners to have to suffer in the name of frugality. The rough edges which had seemed nothing more than par for the course in 1989 had to be ground off.

So part three of the Gemini project (part two being an engine development for trials with the British Army) got under way. The name of the game was technical refinement and, perhaps most importantly, noise – or rather a little less of it. The engine size stayed the same and for the original reasons, in that many export markets imposed swingeing road fund taxes on engines over 2.5 litres. Overall more than 200 components were

changed, including the cylinder head, turbocharger, alternator, pistons/con-rods, and fuel-injectors. As well as the need to compete with the opposition on an equal footing, Land Rover's engineers were also keeping a weather eye on the existing and forthcoming emissions regulations (notably new European regulations due to be enforced in 1996) and great attention was paid to these during the redesign. The result was a success and if it wasn't exactly the smoothest and quietest unit around, it was a great improvement over the 200 Tdi and sales continued apace.

When it came to naming the engines, the 200 Tdi was so-called because its maximum torque was 195lb ft (264Nm); only a little poetic licence was required to make it a 200 prefix. Sadly, the 300 prefix didn't relate to a similar torque figure on the later engine – the queue would have been half-way up the M6! – but to the fact that it was the third phase of the Gemini project.

↓ As the Range Rover's image, equipment level, and price were pushed ever-higher, the Discovery followed suit. The XS was laden with goodies and instantly recognisable thanks to those beautiful, deeply-dished alloy wheels.

CHAPTER 3
BORN AGAIN

Building on the heritage

The Series 2 Discovery was announced by Land Rover on 29 September 1998 – aptly, Land Rover's 50th anniversary year. On sale from 21 November that year, the initial prices ranged from £25,525 for the Td5 base model to £35,095 for the fully equipped V8 ES. It was launched into a market where competition was fierce with popular and impressive vehicles such as Toyota's Landcruiser Colorado, the Mercedes M-Class, Chrysler's Jeep Cherokee and Grand Cherokee, and the Nissan Patrol.

Market research showed that most Discovery owners would be in the 40-plus age group and that many would be driven by women as the 'family car'. It also suggested that the new car would be used mostly out-of-town.

By the time of its introduction, the Discovery was massively successful in 125 markets all over the world, so it was vital to Land Rover that the new model captured new sales but without alienating existing buyers. The S2 was longer and wider, but – following very strong feedback from customer research – retained many of its original styling cues, thus remaining instantly recognisable as a Land Rover product. A quote from the car's chief designer, Alan Mobberley, summed it up: 'The design is the evolution that hides a revolution.'

Despite this, every exterior body panel was new (with the interesting exception of the rear door), with a wider body and track ensuring a stronger overall stance. Not immediately obvious from the outside was a taller windscreen, giving improved forward visibility.

The company invested heavily in new facilities in its Solihull plant in order to maintain and improve build quality standards, already raised to new levels by the Freelander. Initially four models were offered – base, S, XS, and ES – but with only the five-door body style, the three-door not being seen as a

requirement for the typical Discovery buyer. Four trim/equipment levels were offered, all of which boasted driver's air bag, ABS braking, electronic traction control (ETC), and hill descent control (HDC). The three models above base had seven seats and self levelling suspension (SLS), with the top two trim levels adding active cornering enhancement (ACE). (Seven seats, SLS and ACE were optional on other derivatives.)

Inside the car, base and S models had a new cloth trim, with the XS model getting a unique leather and 'Land Rover' fabric combination. The top level ES model had leather-trimmed seats. The driver and front seat passenger were cosseted by new cushion and backrest designs with adjustable armrests, while rear seat passengers had the convenience of a grab-handle built into the front seat headrest.

There were neat features, such as a centre headrest which lowered automatically when the armrest was lowered, offering improved visibility for the driver. An impressive heating/ventilation system was installed as standard on the top-line ES models and was optional on all others. It featured automatic dual-temperature controls with an LCD display for both driver and passenger – just dial in the temperature you require, sit back, and enjoy it.

There was yet more innovation in the 'luggage' area, with very clever folding rear seats, which faced forward and included a retractable headrest – and in common with the other five seats featured three-point seat belts.

All cars had a radio/cassette deck as standard, but there was an upmarket 12-speaker Harman/Kardon 'concert hall' with CD autochanger as an option on S and XS models, and as standard on the ES variant.

← From desert heat to freezing wastes, the Series 2 Discovery was designed to cope with it all. (Nick Dimbleby)

> **DID YOU KNOW?**
> The Series 1 Discovery was never badged as such and neither was the Series 2, until the arrival of the 'facelift' 2003 model, which was launched in 2002. Simple, really!

↑ Launched as a 'lifestyle' vehicle in 1989, the market remained the same nine years later, as can be seen here, with the car heavily accessorised and shown as ideal for the windsurfer and mountain biker. Perhaps Land Rover should also have offered a free session at the gym to help owners cope with all that exercise!

→ The basic dash layout was very similar to the out-going model and, in truth, showed the age of the original design. Where many manufacturers had moved towards one-piece fascia designs, the Discovery still had a component style which tended to look a bit dated; but it was an improvement in terms of ergonomics and suited the rugged luxury appeal of the new vehicle.

Part of this was a neat electronic trick which meant that occupants of the third row of seats could listen through headphones to a different sound source to other vehicle passengers. As the headphone listeners would often be younger children, this was considerably more useful than might at first appear.

Power to the people: the all-new Td5 diesel engine

A major factor in the success of the original Discovery was the Tdi direct injection turbo-diesel engine, which in 200 Tdi and then 300 Tdi forms provided excellent drivability on- and off-road, and a class-leading blend of performance and economy. The Td5 represented a similar leap ahead in 4x4 diesel technology when it made its debut in the Series 2 Discovery.

Developed under the project code name Storm, Land Rover's Td5 was a totally new five-cylinder, 2.5-litre engine aimed at improving on the 300 Tdi's already impressive performance in terms of power, torque, economy, refinement, low cost of ownership, and low emissions. It developed a maximum power of 136bhp and torque of 221lb ft (300Nm), a figure which rose to 232lb ft and 315Nm when coupled to the automatic gearbox option. Diesel engines are all about torque and the maximum figure arrived at just 1,950rpm, but 90 per cent of that was on tap from just 1,450rpm.

The original Project Storm diesel engine concept was approved in 1993, and was for a modular family of four-, five-, and six-cylinder units, the idea being to meet the requirements of both Rover Cars and Land Rover. Development had started when BMW acquired Land Rover in 1994 and continued with its approval. The Td5 was planned to be a specific 4x4 unit to replace the 300 Tdi, the first off the blocks being fitted to the Defender and S2 Discovery.

An important aspect of the new engine was the adoption of electronic unit injector (EUI) technology from Lucas Diesel Systems, giving optimum

↑ ↑ **Given the adverse reaction when the Series 1 facelift car had its indicators moved to the bumper, it seems odd that they were so-sited on the Series 2.**

↑ **Its wider track and more aggressive stance suited the revised Discovery, giving it a really purposeful look.**

performance, refinement, and emissions control. This has been used for many years in premium HGVs and makes for enhanced drivability and economy. EUI uses an individual camshaft-driven plunger pump for each cylinder's injector, with ultra-precise electronic control of the injection period and timing. It can easily provide high injection pressures (the Td5 uses around 22,000psi but 29,000psi is feasible), and because the pressure is only created directly and briefly within the injector itself there are no problems containing the pressure within fuel rails, distribution pipes, or connections, as on other high pressure injection systems. Along with EUI came a newly developed engine control module (ECM), more powerful than any previously available in the Rover Group, petrol or diesel. This major in-house ECM project was code-named Thunder.

One of the Td5's more famous features is its so-called fly-by-wire throttle control. More correctly called fast throttle control (FTC), for road driving

↖ **The hugely impressive Td5 diesel unit was the first of the 'Storm' project's series of modular four-, five-, and six-cylinder engines. The styled acoustic cover fitted over the top of the engine is said to reduce noise levels by 8–10dB (A). There is also an undertray to reduce drive-by noise.**

↑ **What lies beneath the skin is clear in this Land Rover cut-away illustration.**

most of the engine power is accessible in the first 30 per cent of pedal travel, but a more linear, long-travel setting is automatically provided when low-range is selected.

Thor hammers the opposition – quietly

Not to be outdone by a newcomer, the venerable all-aluminium V8 was given no small amount of attention, and was developed under the code name Thor. When compared with the V8 installation in the previous model, the S2 installation had 250.8lb ft (340Nm) of torque, an increase of nine per cent (20.6lb ft or 28Nm), and produced 500rpm lower down the rev range, at 2,600rpm. This was aimed at giving even more effortless acceleration from standstill, and also good response and hill climbing reserve at the motorway cruising speed of 70mph (112kph). The overall torque

spread was also improved, for easier driving on- or off-road; and maximum power went up from 179.7bhp to 182.4bhp, still at 4,750rpm.

Open the bonnet and the most obvious change is the new inlet manifold. Tuned to increase torque, this has twin plenum chambers and long curved induction tracts, exploiting resonance effects for more effective cylinder filling. It is also considerably more compact than the previous 'penthouse' intake plenum, giving improved underbonnet access – and doesn't it just look good?

The engine was blessed with the Bosch Motronic 5.2.1 engine management system, similar to that used on the BMW 7 and 8 Series models. This provided high precision control of the sequential fuel injection and distributorless ignition, with full provision to meet world-wide environmental legislation, including the latest American OBD (on-board diagnostics) requirements. An important aspect of this new ignition package is the adoption of special long-life double platinum (or 'platinum

← The V8 engine came in for yet more revisions under the code name Thor. It was instantly recognisable by the 'bunch of bananas' manifold – more technically, the twin plenum chambers and long curved induction tracts, exploiting resonance effects for more effective cylinder filling. The new unit was more compact than previously, freeing-up valuable underbonnet space.

→ Not unnaturally, Land Rover went to great pains to point out that, despite the many luxury-car fitments, the Discovery was still a competent off-roader. Many press shots showed the cars wading through rivers …

rivet') spark plugs, capable of running maintenance-free for an incredible 72,000 miles (115,800km). Two twin-ignition coils (that's four coils in all) fed two cylinders simultaneously providing the direct ignition according to the ECM programme. New silicon HT leads with high temperature resistance and increased durability were specified. Another new aspect of the engine, and something tried out first on the Freelander, was the returnless fuel rail, with pressure regulation being carried out by a pressure relief valve within the submerged high-pressure fuel pump in the fuel tank. This simplified the fuel system, with the benefit of increased reliability and reduced maintenance.

To increase the robustness and stiffness of the V8, cross-bolted main bearing caps were used (as first introduced for the Range Rover engines) and a new structural cast alloy sump was fitted. The

revised layout for the heater and engine coolant system (including a Td5-like bottom-hose mounted thermostat) necessitated modified rocker covers. There was a new arrangement for driving the front end ancillaries, which included an uprated 130 amp alternator, revised power steering pump, and according to specification, a new swash-plate type air conditioning pump and the new ACE (active cornering enhancement) pump. As on the Td5 diesel, there were four colour-coded poly-vee belts to suit the various permutations of the ancillary serpentine drive. The timing chain cover at the front of the engine was modified to incorporate the oil filler adapter.

Drivetrain

With the new car getting a new diesel engine and refinements for the petrol unit, it seems only fair that the drivetrain also came in for some attention. The R380 five-speed manual gearbox was introduced in 1994 and progressively uprated through the years. For the S2 it was uprated again to cope with the increased torque outputs of both

DID YOU KNOW?

Series 1 Discovery wheels and tyres are largely interchangeable with those from the Series 1 (or Classic) Range Rover – the 90/110/Defender vehicles also use the same wheel stud dimensions. But Series 2 cars have different wheel centres, so are only interchangeable with the Series 2 Range Rover.

engines, with such aspects as an increase in bush sizes and changes to material specifications.

The transfer box was made more robust and quieter (it became the LT230 'Q' because of its lack of noise). A cable selector mechanism replaced the former direct mechanical control for shifting between high and low ranges, giving improved cabin isolation from drive train noise or vibration. The four-speed automatic gearbox was the latest version of the long-standing ZF unit, designated ZF4HP22EH. This featured a sophisticated electronic control to give more precise and consistent gear change points. The transmission control unit (TCU) also communicated with the power unit ECM (petrol or diesel) using a high-speed CANbus link to effect a momentary torque reduction at the point of ratio change, resulting in a smoother change.

The revised 'box operated in two modes: in normal driving, the driver used the selector lever in the conventional manner, through P, R, N, D, and 3, 2, 1 positions in either high or low range. But if the mode selection button was pressed while the road-going high range was in use, a 'Sport' mode was selected, which made more use of available engine power, changing up at higher revs, and changing down more readily. If the same button was pressed whilst low-range was engaged, it changed to 'Manual' mode, which closely emulated a manual transmission, allowing a selected gear (for example 3, 2, or 1) to be held without shifting almost regardless of speed, assisting driver control. In this mode the only situation under which a downshift would then occur would be at very low speed, to avoid stalling the engine.

A further benefit of the new automatic transmission was a comprehensive torque converter lock-up facility. This operated in all gears, and was controlled by the TCU. Using coolant temperature information from the engine management ECM, the TCU calculated a transmission fluid warm-up time from a cold start. Once this time had elapsed, the TCU engaged converter lock-up whenever appropriate – for example when running at steady speeds, to save fuel. However, it would be temporarily disengaged when necessary to smooth a gearshift, and so on. When low range was in use, the lock-up strategy changed to optimise the new Discovery's off-road capabilities. As an example, to provide maximum

↓ ... and scaling the heights around the world. This mountain topper is also a range-topper – the ES model, complete with roof rails, alloy wheels, fog lamps, and protective plastic wheel arch spats.

engine braking, the lock-up would operate even with the throttle closed (again subject only to being disengaged if a potential engine stall situation was detected).

Connecting the gearbox to the source of power, the front propshaft was a new design, with a double Hookes joint at the gearbox end for increased articulation and improved alignment. Last, but certainly not least, was some new axle technology, as used on the S2 Range Rover. The front axle incorporated the 'open yoke' type universal joints that permit a much reduced ground offset for improved steering. The axles had substantially wider tracks (front 1,540mm, rear 1,560mm, compared with 1,486mm front and rear previously) and different bracketry to suit the new suspension arrangements.

Yet another plus point of these complex electronics is that they're able to 'talk' to each other to determine what should be happening and when. For example, when the engine management system adjusts the fuelling to compensate for high altitude conditions, the transmission control likewise adjusts the shift strategy to suit.

Suspension

For techno-enthusiasts, the S2 car was manna from heaven, with electronic widgets abounding. With its active cornering enhancement system, Land Rover claimed an industry first in its declared aim to produce almost car-type road-holding and handling from a large 4x4 off-roader. The system was used in conjunction with self-levelling suspension (SLS) to produce excellent on-road handling and stability, and with the SLS using air springs there was excellent ride comfort and control being maintained over a wide range of load conditions.

For owners who used the massive towing ability of the Discovery, air suspension held other benefits; by using a small hand-held remote control, the rear suspension could be lowered by up to 60mm (2.4in) to align with the trailer hitch. Once connected, the ride could be raised again.

More control of the power train – both on- and off-road – came courtesy of some more complex electronics. Electronic traction control constantly checked all four wheels, braking and releasing where they were spinning without gripping. Hill descent

↑ When out doing a spot of rock climbing, this photo shows the Land Rover trademark of massive axle articulation (see the difference in height between the front wheels) pioneered so well by the Range Rover.

← The epic 'proving' trek continues, note the satellite communications aerial on the leading car. (Nick Dimbleby)

control (HDC), a feature first seen on the smaller Freelander, was fitted, and stopping without locking-up the brakes was given a boost by the installation of electronic brake distribution.

Security

Without doubt, the S2 Discovery was one very attractive proposition and just as much to the thief as the legitimate owner. It was fitting that a hi-tech anti-theft system be installed on the car, based on those in the Range Rover and Freelander. A remote radio key operated the alarm/immobiliser, which featured enhanced volumetric sensors to detect cabin intrusions via broken windows, and a Superlock setting for the door latches, which disabled the interior door handles and sill buttons. Immobilisation and re-mobilisation of the engine was via a simple – but effective – passive transponder in the key. However, the proof of the pudding is in the eating and the acid test came early in 2000, when a team of expert testers attacked 50 of the UK's best-selling cars in order to break in within five minutes. They couldn't get past the Discovery's defences (nor those of the Freelander, also in the same test) and commented that 'Land Rover again comes top of the class, it has consistently refined its security system over the years to the point where Freelander and Discovery are among the most secure models in the entire [50 vehicle] test.' To rub salt in the opposition's wounds, the three other vehicles in that section (one American and two Japanese) took 13.16 seconds, 15.21 seconds and a startling 5.25 seconds to break into.

New star treks over 30,000km to prove a point

In an effort to prove its ruggedness and reliability, a group of journalists from all over the world got together to drive a pair of new Discoverys – a Td5 diesel and a V8 – plus a 1-tonne Ifor Williams trailer, from London to Paris. In essence, not much of a task, but they decided to go the pretty way.

On 1 June 1998 they left London and drove across Western and Eastern Europe, across Turkey, Iran, Pakistan, and India from whence they were shipped to Australia. There, they crossed the dreadfully rutted Gunbarrel Highway to Uluru/Ayers Rock and then on to Melbourne and Sydney. They were then shipped to New York and drove 5,600km (3,480 miles) to central America via New Orleans and Houston, encountering heavy rains as they passed through Guatemala, El Salvador, Honduras, Nicaragua, and Costa Rica. The final boat trip brought the teams back to mainland Europe, landing in Spain and driving up through the Alps in time to show the vehicles at the Discovery premiere at the Paris Show. At various points the teams – and cars – had to cope with daytime temperatures of up to 50° centigrade and nights when it plummeted below freezing, as well as gun-toting militia, ox-carts, camels, monkeys, and unlit overloaded trucks.

And the winner is …

Land Rover has a habit of picking up awards for its cars, and the Discovery II is no exception. In 1999 the Discovery picked up three trophies for its cabinet: *Diesel Car* magazine rated it as Best Diesel

4x4, *Automobile USA* named it the Best Compact Sport Utility, and it was Highly Commended in the Best 4x4 category in *Fleet News*. In its 2000 New Car Honours of the 21st Century, *Auto Express* named the Discovery ES 4-litre V8 as the Best 4x4 off-roader. In the Fleet Excellence awards, *Fleet Management and Business Car* magazine, it won the best 4x4 category.

In the *Auto Express* 2001 honours, the car picked up the trophy for Best 4x4. On this occasion the testers noted that, though the looks had changed little, underneath it was a more rugged machine. They wrote: 'The Disco has become a delight to drive, mainly due to the computer-controlled Active Cornering Enhancement (ACE), which monitors and corrects pitch and roll at all times. No matter what challenges you present it with, the Discovery covers ground with devastating ease. On tarmac, there is a car-like balance between comfortable ride and handling composure which rivals cannot match. Off-road, confidence is the Disco's middle name; even the most greasy mud-banks are child's play. Hill Descent Control (HDC) linked to the electronic traction, along with ABS braking systems, are responsible for this. A prestige badge helps but, when it comes to taking the rough with the smooth, there really is nothing to beat the Discovery.' I think

↑ Inside, the Autobiography's specifications went off the end of the scale. The antithesis of the original Discovery, now the company offered any colour you liked – as long as it was any colour you liked!

← By 2001 the Series 2 was being pushed ever higher in terms of equipment and, of course, price. Mirroring the Range Rover, the Autobiography cars were launched at the UK Motor Show. The aim was to offer customers the option of having just about any specification they wanted, from the style of alloy wheel to the colour of the mirrors.

it's fair to say that they liked it. Also in 2001, the V8 model was named Middleweight 4x4 of the Year by *Off Road and 4 Wheel Drive* magazine. A year later, *Auto Express* voted it the Best Used 4x4, making the car a winner regardless of age.

The 2003 Discovery: the L318

As has become de rigueur with the modern car industry, vehicles get a facelift about halfway through their production cycle. As such, it was no surprise to find the Series 2 car getting one, although Land Rover insisted on calling it the Discovery 2003, despite the fact it went on sale on 1 June 2002. The car was first shown to the public on 27 March 2002, at the New York International Auto Show.

The factory reference was L318 and as facelifts go, this was far more than a nip and tuck to keep things smart, though as Land Rover had stumped up a steady £24 million, you'd expect a little more than a paint change and bumper redesign. In fact, there were more than 700 major and detail changes, notably:

- A distinctive new 'face', inspired by the new Range Rover.
- Revised rear lights for extra safety.
- A new centre differential lock for greater off-road ability.
- Prestigious new interior colours.
- New thicker-style roof bars.
- New front bumper with an increased step height.
- Braking and suspension improvements.
- A new 4.6-litre V8 engine (for the North American market only).

Commenting on the new Discovery, the managing director of Land Rover UK, Mike Wright, said: 'The Discovery is already the best-selling large 4x4 in the UK. It has dominated that market since the original model was launched and we're confident that, with the latest round of improvements, customers will continue to be attracted to this practical and versatile vehicle.'

Prices for the new Discovery were unchanged from the previous model, and began at £21,995 for the Td5 E and rose to £34,490 for the 4.0-litre V8 ES.

Pre-production testing

Pre-production testing is a vital part of preparing any new car and the Discovery 2003 underwent more exhaustive testing than any previous example of the model, with the vehicle often being 'real-world' tested alongside the new Range Rover during the latter's development programme. Special prominence was placed on hot environment testing, reflecting the Discovery's popularity in Gulf and North American markets. Here heat management issues came to the fore, with new heat shields and air deflectors being developed for the vehicle, especially in connection with the availability of the 4.6-litre V8 engine for North America (see below).

Design

After agonising over the Series 1 design in 1989, drawing up the Series 2 in 1998 was somewhat easier because they had already had experience of replacing a style icon – the Range Rover, in 1994. Though the 2003 was bigger and very different to the original car, the company kept the distinctive profile; it was quite obviously a Discovery and retained all the styling cues which had made the original so popular – the upright stance, commanding driving position, low shoulder line, simple grille and short overhangs front and rear for good approach and departure angles off-road.

The front-end styling was radically different, clearly derived from the S3 Range Rover, and was probably the most noticeable feature of the 2003. Central to the new look were the 'pocketed' headlamps with twin interlocking dip and main beam projectors, visible behind a clear lens. The headlamp assembly was completed by smaller indicator and parking lights on the outside edge of the unit. Whilst it benefited the company to create a Rover 'family' link between Discovery and Range Rover, the new lamps also had practical and safety implications, providing far better performance in terms of the spread and range of the beam and in the evenness of the illumination. The new lights sat either side of a new, three-bar elongated grille, beneath which was a revised three-piece bumper which had circular fog lamps inset towards the outer edges. By mounting the lamps slightly higher than previously, they became less prone to damage, whether on- or off-road. The

↓ Those trendy – and effective – headlamp clusters instantly mark this Series 2 car as a 'facelift' model. Compare it with …

profile of the bumper was adapted to improve the off-road abilities of the car, with the easily-replaceable end caps being painted black or body colour (depending on specification).

There were fewer obvious revisions at the rear; the indicators were enlarged and moved from their previous position within the rear bumper assembly to the main light cluster housing, in the rear pillars flanking the tailgate. The reversing lights were housed in the rear bumper display alongside the high intensity rear fog lamps.

Chassis

The 2003 Discovery featured six cross members and no fewer than 14 body mounting points, its stiff construction being the anchor for the dynamic control systems that gave the 2003 its on-road control/refinement and off-road ability. Wide track beam axles had lateral location by a Watts linkage at the rear and by a Panhard rod at the front. Vertical location was by radius arms pivoting on low friction bushes. Revised front suspension geometry included an optimised ride height to improve cornering composure and steering precision. The front axle used open yoke universal joints, giving accurate steering response and a tight turning circle. The power assisted worm and roller steering was also revised to enhance feedback and on-road accuracy still further.

Making any vehicle as competent on-road as it is off-road takes some doing, but the 2003 Discovery achieved it by using some of the most sophisticated electronic chassis control systems in the world. As on the outgoing model, ACE was used to give car-like handling attributes despite the vehicle's size. The system is operated by quick-reacting hydraulic actuators powered by a high pressure pump. The actuators automatically stiffen the suspension, guided by an electronic control unit taking information from vehicle-mounted sensors. This results in a reduction in body roll in cornering, giving extra driver confidence and passenger comfort.

← ... the Series 3 Range Rover and it's obvious where the inspiration came from. Having a family connection with the largest, most luxurious – and most expensive – off-roader Land Rover has ever made doesn't do any harm to the Discovery's upmarket image.

↓ Though most of the initial batch of photos showed the new car in light colours, predominantly silver, there's no doubt that dark colours give the 2003 a lick of real style.

↑ At the rear, the changes
were subtle. The lamp
clusters were raised and
the indicators were moved
from their former position
in the bumpers, which now
housed the large reversing
lamps and fog lamps.

ACE functions off-road, too, because the
control unit can detect off-road driving patterns
and automatically adjust the suspension to allow
greater articulation, giving extra agility. On side
slopes the ACE system locks the suspension for
improved confidence. This innovative and intelligent
system is a no-compromise approach, giving agile
on-road handling without compromising off-road
performance.

Because the Discovery had the ability to carry
up to seven passengers, carry a large payload, and
tow up to 3,500kg (3.4 tons), lots of thought was
given to keeping it on an even keel; any vehicle which
ends up with its nose pointing in the air when coping
with a heavy load is inherently unstable, lacking
in braking power, and the headlamps are likely to
dazzle oncoming road-users. The 2003 featured
self-levelling suspension, using air springs in the rear
suspension system fed by an electronically-controlled
compressor. Sensors detect vehicle attitude and
adjust the suspension to maintain a level position,
regardless of load. Self-levelling avoids the need to
use stiffer springing, preserving smooth ride comfort.

Another feature of the air suspension is that by
pressing a fascia button when off-road, the body is
raised to provide extra clearance at the rear and
increase departure angles. And should the 2003
ground at low speed when off-road, sensors will
detect a spinning rear wheel and automatically raise

the rear springs to help lift the vehicle out of trouble.
A further function allows the rear of the vehicle to
be lowered to facilitate the hitching of a trailer.

Certain versions of the 2003 Discovery were
available with coil-spring suspension all round. As well
as improving tolerances, changes included a wider
variety of spring rates so that reaction to vehicle
mass could be optimised across a wider range of
equipment specifications.

Exterior

On the outside, there was a new selection of rather
nice (and expensive) alloy wheels, including new five-
and six-spoke 16-inch wheels and a pair of 18-inch
wheels styles. Regardless of wheel choice, Land Rover
made great efforts to reduce the effect of radial force
variation (RFV) caused by out-of-balance wheels and
tyres. No matter how accurate conventional wheel
balancing is, there is still some imbalance between
wheel and tyre. And of course, it is rare for the
wheel and tyre assemblies at either end of the same
axle to be in perfect harmony with one another.
Even perfectly balanced assemblies tend to go out of
balance once they have been used on a vehicle. To try
and overcome RFV problems on the Discovery 2003,
wheels and tyres were not only balanced to each
other, but also bedded down as an assembly before

→ This seriously luxurious
interior is a long way from
the acres of Sonar Blue
that graced those first
models.

they got to the production line – including the spare. As such, they were in balance from the outset and would stay so even after the vehicle had been driven.

Worries about the cost of replacing bits of the rear end during a parking shunt could be alleviated by stumping up around £250 for the park distance control (PDC) option on the GS and XS models. This was standard on the ES.

Up on top, new roof bars with a thicker profile could be specified, which as well as being a practical load-carrying feature, helped define the look of the 2003 Discovery.

Interior

Three new trim colours were introduced: Tundra Green, Alpaca Beige and Land Rover Black. More importantly, the seal fit of doors and windows was overhauled in an effort to reduce wind noise and water ingress. Changes in production techniques and tolerances improved the panel fit and other NVH (noise, vibration and harshness) issues were addressed by changes to the air induction system – a second resonator was added to the system to quieten induction roar.

Improvements in the materials used in the interior minimised squeaks and rattles and the

company claimed that quality improvements on the production line dramatically lowered the level of faults per vehicle.

In line with its upmarket image, those with enough cash could specify an on-board DVD player which could be viewed (by rear seat passengers only) on a roof-mounted screen.

↑ Those rather dubious-quality plastics have also disappeared; but the seat design very much retains the look of the original car, particularly with the distinctive head-rest arrangement.

→ Not exactly straight off the production line, and those ladies certainly aren't on the official options list! Silly it may be, but there's a serious and good cause behind it: sponsored by Goodyear, an all-women team drove a new 2003 model diesel Land Rover Discovery in the Trans World Events 'Midnight Sun to Red Sea' rally on behalf of Cancer Research UK, for which £100,000 was raised. The event started from Ostersund in Sweden on 1 June and finished in Aqaba, Jordan, on 21 June. To raise extra sponsorship cash, the car was christened with a kiss by a whole host of caring stars, including Patsy Kensit, Kate Winslet, Darcey Bussell, Jerry Hall, Tania Bryer, Jemima Khan, Jilly Cooper, Faye Tozer and Twiggy. The rather striking Discovery livery included a giant pink lipstick mark, a flashing pair of 'eyelashes' on the headlights and celebrity signatures.

Engines

There was no change under the bonnet for the 2003 Discovery. With the five-cylinder, 137bhp 2.5-litre Td5 turbo diesel engine accounting for a staggering 95 per cent of all Series 2 UK sales, it was no surprise to find it retaining its position in the new car. For those with deeper pockets, the 4.0-litre 185bhp V8 was still available. And if it wasn't bad enough that our North American cousins paid peanuts for petrol, they also got an option of the ex-Series 2 Range Rover 4.6-litre V8 engine, producing a steady 220bhp.

Brakes and drivetrain

The drivetrain of the 2003 model was essentially unchanged, being a permanent four-wheel drive set-up, with separate transfer box and a choice of five-speed manual or four-speed automatic gearboxes (the latter being standard on the V8-engined models). The ZF auto 'box has dual mode operation. This electronically controlled unit

features a high-speed digital link with the engine management system to ensure gear-changes are swift and precise. The dual mode function provides for a Sport mode in high range that alters throttle response for a more reactive feel. In low range a Manual mode is available, enabling a selected gear to be held without shifting, allowing the driver greater control to negotiate a wide range of off-road conditions.

The transfer box featured extra ribbing on the case, revised mounting points and new mesh gear patterns, the aim being to lower NVH intrusion, while extensive use was made of new damping panels to prevent body-generated boom. The high/low shift is operated by a remote, cable-operated control that isolates the vehicle interior from the transmission to improve refinement. Off-roaders were delighted to find that a locking centre differential had reappeared, to augment the electronic traction control system.

Standard on all models was a four-channel anti-lock braking system (ABS), incorporating electronic brakeforce distribution (EBD) that adjusts the braking to suit the vehicle load condition, optimising the braking effect. Naturally, discs were fitted at each corner; these had new pads and a revised master cylinder with revised stroke. Coupled with changes to the brake calliper piston and modifications to the ABS control programme, the new brake system had improved sensitivity, pedal travel and feel.

Allied to the ABS system, the 2003 was also fitted with four-wheel electronic traction control as standard. This system has dual mode functionality for on- and off-road environments, increasing driver confidence in all conditions. A new master cylinder and revised pad material combine to shorten pedal travel and give more feel, especially under heavy braking.

The 2003 was fitted with hill descent control (HDC) as standard. First seen on the Land Rover Freelander (and also on the Series 3 Range Rover), it supplements normal engine braking while descending steep slopes off-road. It operates only in low range, applying the brakes to slow the vehicle and thereby maintaining maximum control. (HDC was granted the Queen's Award for Enterprise: Innovation in 2001.)

↑ **Given the projected export markets for the new car, a great deal of attention was paid to testing in hot and humid climates. New heat shields and air deflectors were developed as a direct result.**

← **Despite making much of the 2003's on-road abilities, Land Rover was very keen to stress that the Discovery is still very much an off-road tool. Those test drivers just can't keep out of the water!**

CHAPTER 4
DISCO 3 – THE THIRD GENERATION

Although popular, the Discovery MKII, introduced in 1989, relied on a very old design – the chassis/body layout being essentially that of the first Range Rover introduced in 1970, which in general principle went back as far as the first Series 1 Land Rover. So, to compete with the Japanese and European opposition, which had become seriously 21st century, the new Discovery had to follow the lead of its Range Rover sibling and burst through into the third millennium. The Discovery 3 was launched in the UK in November 2004 and, whilst instantly recognisable as a Land Rover product, nothing at all was carried over from the previous model. In the USA, where the MKII had got itself a reputation for poor reliability, it was rebranded as the Land Rover LR3.

UK launch prices started at £26,995 for the TDV6 5-seater and from there, via a catalogue of options and a V8 engine, to £46,995 for the top-range HSE 7-seater. In the USA, $44,995 was the base price for the only model initially available (the V8 of course) but it took only a few extras to boost that to well over $50,000.

The Discovery 3 was the first vehicle wholly developed by the new management team that took over Land Rover in July 2000 (following the purchase by Ford Motor Company). Its aim was not just to do everything better than the outgoing model, but also to improve on anything the competition could offer. MD Matthew Taylor said, 'The Discovery 3 is a new generation Land Rover, a vehicle of great conviction that points the way forward for the company. As you would expect from a Land Rover, it is awesome off-road. What may be more surprising to some is its great performance on-road too. The result is the widest breadth of capability in the class.'

Design

The design goal for the Discovery 3 was simple. To produce a modern vehicle that offered maximum cabin space and versatility but would be instantly recognisable as a Land Rover.

According to Land Rover's design director Geoff Upex, the vehicle was designed from the inside out. He said, 'Our priorities were cabin space, comfort, the Command driving position, and elevated "stadium seating" in the rear. The exterior design is a reflection of those interior priorities. It is very geometric, very minimalist, very modern. Everything is there for a reason. It is pure product design, rather than fancy automotive styling. The best vehicles inevitably are. It is also distinctively Land Rover. You won't confuse this vehicle with anything else.'

The latter was certainly true because the lack of a side styling swage gave the car a unique, rather slab-sided, look which aroused public comment and divided opinion between the Land Rover official line as previously, and those who rather cruelly compared it to large commercial vehicles. The official response is that a side styling line was considered superfluous and so was rejected! 'It was an area of comment in preview clinics with potential customers,' says Upex. 'Most cars have side styling lines, so people expect them. But we found the more people looked at, and became familiar with, the Discovery 3, the more they liked it and "got it". There was similar comment about the car only having one side air intake. "Why not two?", people asked. Simple – it only needs one. So it only has one.'

Structure

The body of the Discovery 3 was a combination of steel, much of which is high-strength grade, and

← Much of the mud 'n' ruts pre-launch testing was carried out in the UK. This shot is at Eastnor Castle in Herefordshire, but the car went all round the world and was subjected to all manner of extreme conditions. (Nick Dimbleby)

DID YOU KNOW?
The rather impressive 6-cylinder diesel engine as fitted to the Discovery is also used in some models of Ford Mondeo and the Citroen C5 (though obviously some changes are made to suit those very different vehicles).

aluminium. Unlike most bodies attached to separate platforms, the Discovery 3 body is a key part of the structure. This match of rigid body and strong platform gives Land Rover's all-new Integrated Body-frame (IBF) structure its stiffness and its strength. This innovative vehicle architecture combined the torsional rigidity, car-like handling, and refinement of a monocoque body, with the strength and versatility of a traditional ladder-frame.

As well as handling precision, driving refinement, ride, and comfort, it also helped reduce shakes and rattles. Although it had much greater cabin space, the Discovery 3 was only 176mm (around 7in) longer than the outgoing Discovery model, and 30mm (1.25in) wider.

Computer-aided design, high-strength steel, and a sophisticated hydroforming technique combined to deliver this new technology. (Hydroforming uses high-pressure fluids rather than a press tool to shape the frame, which results in lighter weight, cleverer shapes, and much tighter tolerances.)

The Discovery 3's body was manufactured like a conventional monocoque with two monosides welded to the floor, roof, and bulkheads, creating a strong, single structure. Enormously strong boron steel is used for the A- and B-pillars for added strength in front and side impacts. The roof structure was designed to accommodate both a sunroof and alpine roof – an essential part of the Discovery design carried over from the very first models. The sunroof was a conventional cassette-type design, opening rearwards, outside the vehicle. The alpine

→ **The stylish interior is a very pleasant place to be – created to be practical but luxurious, as in its bigger brother the Range Rover. (Nick Dimbleby)**

↘ **Opinion was divided from the off about the 'missing' side swage line. The designers kept the stepped roof from the original, and the glass area was massive, giving an airy feel for up to seven occupants. (Land Rover)**

↓ **The ifs, buts, and maybes of the design gestation required a shape that harked back to Land Rover's heritage but looked forward to the new century. Here's a handful of sketches from the final stages. (Nick Dimbleby)**

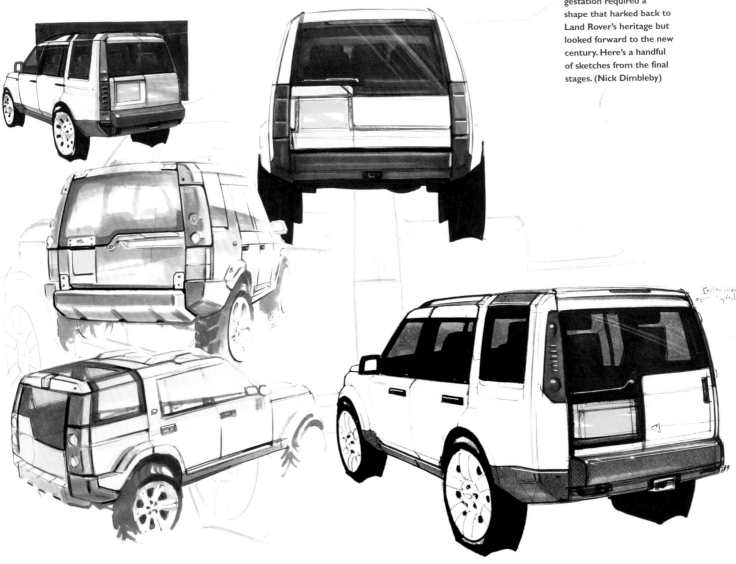

roof was a large, full-width glass roof bonded into the metal structure, above the second and third-row seats. To preserve strength, it was braced by cross members, invisible from the outside.

When neither the sunroof nor the alpine roof option was selected, the outer roof panel was a single large steel pressing with styled swages to add strength and prevent 'booming'. The tailgate, doors, bonnet, and front wings were separate bolt-on assemblies, with lightweight magnesium alloy used for part of the front structure and forming part of the front crash crumple zone.

The bonnet, with its characteristic Land Rover clamshell design, was aluminium to save weight (and make opening and closing easier) and utilised gas struts to provide assistance and retain the bonnet in the open position. The hinge allowed the bonnet to be locked vertically for easier access to the engine compartment during servicing.

At the rear, the asymmetric tailgate was a two-piece design, similar to that of the Range Rover. The lower half opened downwards and the top half upwards – a design feature which improved reach-in distance and helped with loading large or heavy objects. With the vehicle stationary, the upper

tailgate could be closed independently of the lower tailgate, partly enclosing the vehicle interior while the lower tailgate could be used, for example, as a viewing platform. The lower tailgate also served as an acoustic chamber for the sub-woofer (where fitted) – part of the in-car entertainment system. Both upper and lower tailgates were made from lightweight aluminium, which helped reduce total vehicle mass and also made opening and closing easier. The spare wheel moved to a new home under the body, rather than on the rear door.

All four doors were wide for easy access. Made of steel, they had boron steel-reinforced side intrusion beams to improve impact performance. The front and rear bumpers, end trims, sill finishers, and wheel arch eyebrows were all polypropylene injection mouldings designed to brush off minor damage in normal and off-road driving. Both bumpers had energy-absorbing elements to protect vital components in low speed impacts.

Once completed, the body was subjected to a comprehensive painting and finishing process to ensure it retained an attractive appearance throughout its long life. All steel panels vulnerable to corrosion were zinc coated. Alloy structures, inherently corrosion-resistant, were treated to prevent electrolytic interaction with adjoining steel components, the bane of many an earlier Discovery owner. The body was finished in what was claimed to be one of the most environmentally-friendly and advanced paint facilities in the world.

Lighting the way

The headlamp lenses were moulded in damage-resistant polycarbonate. Entry-level models featured twin-pocket halogen headlamps, whilst the mid-line system used bi-function xenon projectors with auxiliary halogen main beam lamps. Optional fixed cornering lamps were also available (except for the USA).

High-level models got an adaptive front lighting system (AFS). Linked to the vehicle's sophisticated electrical architecture, AFS receives information on vehicle speed, steering angle, axle position, and gear selection. Analysing this information, the projectors swivel left or right accordingly. Additional static bending lights (again not in the USA) were mounted at 45 degrees to the car line to give extra light to the

↑ Said to have been designed 'from the inside out', the Stadium Seating was one of the cornerstones of the new car, the seven-seater option being incredibly popular and …

direction in which the car is turning. They were also illuminated at low speed to assist with manoeuvring or parking. AFS also features dynamic levelling to allow for different load weights and position. The front lights were protected by tough polycarbonate covers with pressure wash as an option. The rear lights were mounted high on the rear corner pillars for good visibility.

Interior

Though externally not much bigger than the outgoing model, the Discovery 3 was roomier inside, featuring a spacious cabin packed with clever stowage locations and very versatile seating arrangements. 'The cabin was the starting point for the creation of the Discovery 3,' said Geoff Upex. 'Maximum cabin space and comfort dictated the entire form of the vehicle.'

In every major dimension, the new vehicle's interior was either class-leading or among the best. Compared with the outgoing Discovery model, the major improvements were in leg room, shoulder room, and third-row headroom. The third row of seats (where fitted) were extremely spacious – large enough for 95th percentile adults – and the wide doors ensured easy cabin and boot access.

The second and third seat rows could fold right down into the floor, enabling the car to transform into a luxury load-carrier with a flat floor and huge capacity – almost two metres long.

The vehicle could be specified with either two or three rows of seats, giving space for five or seven adults respectively. All seats faced forwards and provided a head restraint and full lap-and-diagonal inertia-reel seat belt. 'Stadium seating' in this instance meant that each row was higher than the one in front, improving the view for all passengers, something helped by the deep glazing and the stepped roof, which ensured plenty of headroom for all passengers.

All seats were large and comfortable, the higher-level Discovery 3 models coming with leather upholstery, and the outer seats in the second row were equipped with Isofix attachment points for European-standard and North American child seats.

Those in the front were truly spoilt for choice as the seats were available with power adjustment, covering fore and aft movement, height and squab recline, plus manual lumbar support adjustment. In addition, the driver's seat offered electric cushion tilt adjustment. On manual front seats there were fore and aft adjustment and squab recline, plus lumbar support and height adjust on the driver's seat. In the five-seat version, the rear seats split asymmetrically (65:35) and were folded by lifting the lower cushions and moving the squabs forward, to give a flat loading deck.

In the seven-seat version, the second row of seats featured three individual seats, each of which folded separately and retracted into the footwell. The two outer seats could also 'jack-knife' forward for easy access to the third-row seats. The individual folding

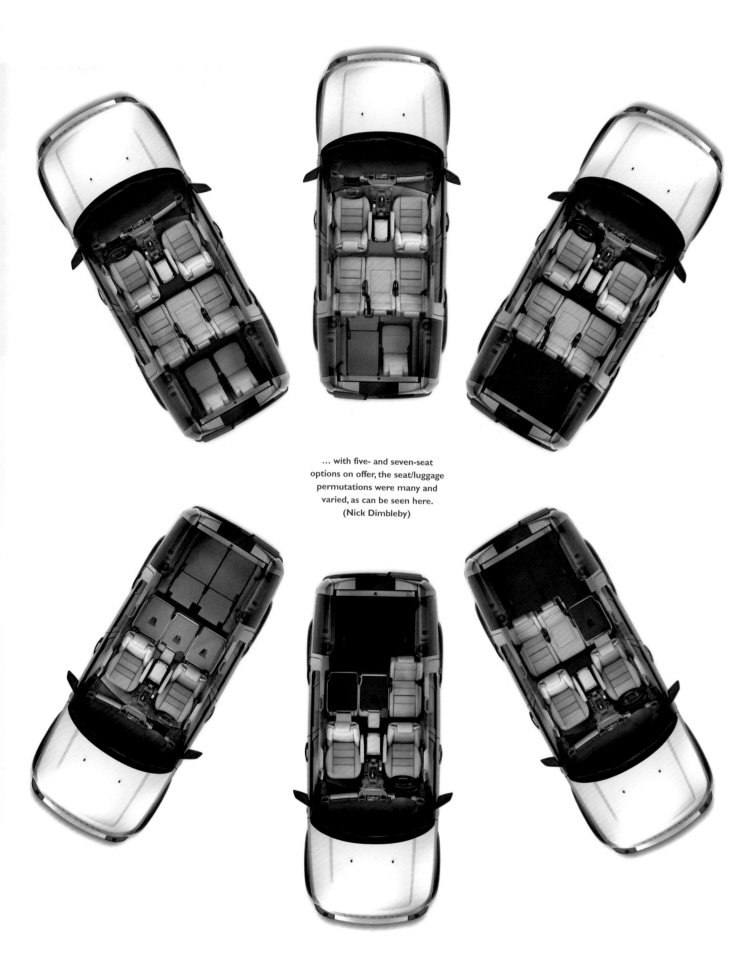

... with five- and seven-seat options on offer, the seat/luggage permutations were many and varied, as can be seen here. (Nick Dimbleby)

arrangements for all five rear seats provided anything from a two-seat to a seven-seat vehicle, with varying formats of load space.

Extensive stowage space was a priority; in the facia there were two gloveboxes on the passenger side, a tray at the base of the front console with a non-slip mat and a coin tray, and clip for tickets and toll slips.

The use of an Electronic Park Brake (rather than a cumbersome conventional handbrake lever) created extra space in the centre console. As such, a large cubby box, which could hold up to four drink cans, was fitted right behind the console, and this was available with a cooling system to keep drinks chilled. The cubby box lid could be folded back to act as a useful tray for rear-seat passengers. It could also be used to stow a mobile phone which could be integrated into a hands-free system.

Large cup-holders for driver and front seat passenger were fitted in the centre console, and there was an additional folding cup-holder for the passenger.

Both front doors had capacious bins, including holders for larger bottles. The rear side doors also had large bins, again big enough for drink bottles – in all, 17.5 litres of drinks could be stowed.

Large lower quarter panels in the rear compartment provided stowage space for those sitting in the third row, or secure stowage in the boot area. The top surface included a cup-holder and shallow tray, as well as in-car entertainment controls for the rear-seat passengers. Recesses, closed with nets, were also offered for extra stowage.

The Facia

The facia had a simple, geometric look, utilising the Land Rover styling from the contemporary Range Rover, with clear vertical and horizontal lines. There was large instrumentation, plus good-sized, tactile, and intuitive controls. Switches were deliberately kept to a minimum, especially as the built-in technology (such as the Terrain Response system) can do much of the work for the driver without additional input.

The facia moulding was made from Thermoplastic Urethane (TPU), which had a luxury feel, resisted fade caused by sunlight, and had fewer plasticisers (to reduce the mist deposited on the inside of the windscreen). The facia was supported on a die-cast magnesium alloy cross-beam (both light and strong),

↓ The much-lauded Terrain Response System (TRS) made getting the right gear/differential/ride-height a breeze, especially when … (Nick Dimbleby)

← … the state of play was clearly denoted by a series of pictograms on the satnav display. However, the actual technicalities of the system … (Nick Dimbleby)

↗ … are rather more complex, as can be seen in this cutaway through the front of the floor pan. (Nick Dimbleby)

→ The electronics systems within the Discovery 3 require huge amounts of cabling, even despite the use of canbus. Note also the huge catalytic converter. (Nick Dimbleby)

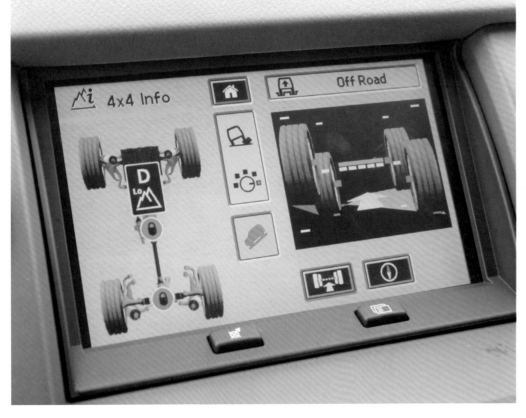

which provided precise mounting and reduced a propensity to rattle.

The top panel for the facia was designed to look and feel good, and regularly used controls (such as facia vents) typically had a rubberised finish to improve touch, and boost their premium feel.

The roof and door pillar trim were soft fabric, and all grab handles were damped, which always gives a luxury feel. Two roof-mounted consoles provided interior lighting, with separate lights for the third-row passengers. Low-level 'waterfall' lighting was incorporated into the front dome lamp, and was activated when the headlamps were turned on. When the alpine roof was specified, full width blinds provided shade and extra privacy. Carpets were soft but necessarily hard-wearing. Sweeping out was made easier by the sill-free body design.

As one would expect, air-conditioning was standard on all models and came in two formats; manually-operated and automatic. Both included a particulate filter to remove pollutants in both fresh-air and recirculating modes, and four facia-mounted adjustable vents with thumbwheel shut-offs. There was an additional lap cooler vent for the driver beneath the steering wheel. Airflow was also

directed at the windscreen, side windows, and front footwells. For the second row of seats, there were two vents at the back of the centre console.

On higher level vehicles, fully automatic temperature control was used. This system automatically used the air-conditioning and heater to maintain a constant temperature. The temperature was selected using separate facia-mounted controls for driver and passenger. Both sides operated independently. (In selected hot-weather markets, the system could be specified with optional rear air-conditioning and heating. In cold-weather markets, an additional 5kW fuel-burning heater supplemented the heat generated by the TDV6 diesel engine.)

Multimedia and information

Gone are the days when a simple radio was on the options list – the Discovery 3 was offered with a dizzying range of multimedia arrangements to rival most multiplex cinemas. Higher-line models came with a six-CD in-dash unit, with base-spec cars

getting six speakers and upper range models having more powerful Harman/Kardon systems with nine speakers, including a sub-woofer for really impressive bass reproduction.

A premium 14-speaker Harman/Kardon Logic 7 seven-channel digital surround system was also available with a head unit which could also play MP3 files and, with 11 times compression, the equivalent of a 66 disc CD library could be stored and played in the vehicle.

The optional DVD navigation system included Traffic Message Channel (TMC), which broadcasts messages on a specific radio channel to warn of hold-ups. This information is also shown on-screen, and the navigation system can suggest an alternative route to ensure the driver has an uninterrupted journey.

The navigation system was controlled by a 180mm (7in) high-resolution touch screen, whilst two buttons switched the screen between the main 'Home' menu and the navigation system. Voice recognition was available for navigation and audio controls, and the screen also showed information from the Terrain Response system.

Safety

The enormously strong Integrated Body-frame architecture of the Discovery 3, with its hydroformed frame, gave tremendous protection in case of impacts, and door-mounted anti-intrusion side-beams offered further protection. Passenger safety was improved by the use of up to eight airbags. The driver's airbag was installed in the steering-wheel boss and the front passenger airbag in the facia, while two airbags in the front seats provided protection for the thorax. There were two full-length curtain airbags fitted in the cant rails above the first and second rows of seats, offering side protection. When seven seats were specified, two additional side bags were fitted in the rearmost area.

Engines

PETROL V8

As you would expect, the top-of-the-range engine option was a petrol-fuelled V8, in this case a 4.4-litre unit derived from Jaguar's acclaimed AJ-V8 4.2-litre engine (via an increase in bore size from 86 to 88mm) which produced 295bhp (220kW). Though this was slightly less than when used in the equivalent Jaguar XK, XJ or X-Type, the power arrived 500rpm earlier, at 5,500rpm. In line with the car's need for low-end pulling power, the engine electronic mapping was reworked to produce a healthy 315lb ft (425Nm) of torque at just 4,000rpm. This made it the most powerful unit ever fitted to a production Land Rover, and the technically impressive quad-cam (double overhead camshafts per bank) 32-valve unit was one of the world's lightest V8s, due to its compact dimensions and use of lightweight aluminium alloy block and heads. In addition, it was also renowned for its thermal efficiency, which resulted in improved economy from quicker warm-up times. The engine used an electronic throttle and Variable Camshaft Phasing (VCP) – which automatically and continuously controlled valve timing according to driving demands and outside temperature.

In addition, it had greater weather-proofing (especially against dust and water ingress) and revised breathing for wading in rivers. From the off, this was the only engine available in America, where low fuel prices make a nonsense out of buying a diesel-engined car.

Because the Discovery 3 could well be working at some odd angles – especially compared with its Jaguar cousins – the oil capacity was significantly increased, from 6.8 litres to 8.6 litres. The oil pump was new, for improved delivery, and the front crank oil seal was also modified to guard against the ingress of water, mud or slurry during wading or other off-road conditions. The aluminium oil sump was also new, and engine ancillaries were repositioned as high as possible to prevent the possibility of damage when off-road.

TDV6 DIESEL

In over-taxed Europe, hopes were pinned firmly to the refined and flexible 2.7-litre TDV6 turbo diesel unit that used variable geometry turbocharging.

↑ ↑ **Top of the engine range was this, the 4.4 litre V8 monster, developed from the unit that powered sporty Jaguars (at the time part of Ford), and producing 295bhp and 315lb ft of torque. However, the big seller ... (Nick Dimbleby)**

↑ **... in over-taxed Britain was unsurprisingly the impressive 2.7 litre TDV6 turbo-diesel. Though down on power with 190bhp, it actually had more torque with 325lb ft. The sound-deadening covers hide most of it ... (Nick Dimbleby)**

↑ ... so here's what
it looks like before
installation. As elsewhere,
technical innovation
abounds, though for the
sake of more torque a
single KKK turbocharger
was used, rather than
two as on the Jaguar
application. (Land Rover)

(Another version of this new V6 had recently made its debut in the Jaguar S-Type.) The unit utilised common rail technology, operating at some 25 per cent greater pressure than average, which benefited performance, economy, and emissions. Another technological innovation was the use of a compacted graphite iron (CGI) engine block – one of the first uses of this material in volume engine production. CGI is stronger, stiffer, lighter, and more durable than cast iron, from which diesel engine blocks are usually manufactured. This inherent stiffness worked elsewhere, improving driving refinement, and its strength and lightness meant the engine required less mass, and thus had smaller dimensions than a traditional V6 turbo diesel. The stiffness and strength

also removed the need for cylinder liners, and the cylinders were bored directly into the block casting, a further and very welcome weight-saving. The cylinder heads were pressure die cast in aluminium alloy, each featuring twin overhead camshafts operating four valves per cylinder. The camshafts were driven by a flexible belt coated in PTFE to reduce friction. To increase both reliability and precision, the camshaft belts weren't required to drive any other system (such as power steering, etc.). Unlike the derivative used in Jaguars, the TDV6 turbodiesel had an aluminium ladder-frame at the bottom of the crankcase, to improve rigidity. Its baffle plates prevented oil foaming and surging when off-road. Attached to the ladder-frame was a pressed-steel sump. The oil pick-up point was optimally designed to operate at acute off-road angles. The compression ratio of 17.3:1 was relatively low for a diesel engine, but this was designed to reduce heat build-up in the piston bowl, which in turn improved fuel-burning efficiency and reduced fuel consumption and emissions. A reduction in engine noise was a welcome side-effect.

The inlet manifold was made from composite material, moulded integrally with the cam covers, and isolated from the cylinder heads by an elastomeric material to reduce vibration. Each cylinder featured twin inlet ports, one being a 'filling' port, designed to get as much air as possible into the cylinder, whilst the other was a helical 'swirl' port to generate the vortices necessary for optimum fuel combustion. In certain part-load conditions, the engine management system would close the 'filling' port to increase the swirl effect. This altered the combustion characteristics, reducing emissions and noise. The engine control unit (ECU) was also unique to Land Rover and collated information input from over 20 sensors around the engine. As had become de rigueur for any powerful diesel unit, the TDV6 was turbocharged, in this case by a single, fully sealed (to suit wading) KKK unit for optimum torque – the equivalent Jaguar engine had twin turbochargers. The turbo used an electronically controlled Variable Nozzle Turbine to ensure air delivery was optimised by altering the angle of the turbine vanes. This effectively widened the turbine inlet at low speed to improve torque, and narrowed it at high speed for better power response – the best of both worlds. The engine had a glow plug in each cylinder to assist in cold starts. In terms of emissions, it easily met the then current EU3 emissions legislation and had the potential to satisfy all known future legislation. The maximum power was 190bhp (140kW) at 4000rpm, and maximum torque was an enormous 440Nm (325lb ft), developed at a mere 1900rpm.

V6 PETROL

Not available in the UK, a 4.0-litre petrol V6 engine was available in some markets. Its aim, as with the older 4.0-litre V8 engine, was to offer a reasonable compromise between economy and performance. The 215bhp (160kW) was 13 per cent more than the 4.0-litre V8, whilst the torque figure of 265lb ft (360Nm) was certainly substantial. The Ford-derived engine used a cast-iron block with aluminium-alloy heads and a counter-balanced crankshaft for extra refinement. As ever, extensive modifications were required to tailor the engine for specific 4 x 4 use. There was a die-cast aluminium ladder-frame on

the bottom of the block to stiffen the structure, with baffle plates to stop surge and oil foaming. The revised sump included a new oil pick-up pipe to improve lubrication at all angles. The alternator, air-conditioning compressor, and power-steering pump were all unique to Land Rover, and were positioned as high as possible to keep them out of harm's way during extreme off-roading.

A new cast aluminium variable-tract inlet manifold was developed specifically for the Discovery 3. Controlled by a new engine management system, it improved torque and driving characteristics. The lower profile manifold also helped keep things neat and compact under the bonnet. The electronically-controlled throttle regulated torque delivery and was linked to Land Rover's patented Terrain Response system, which constantly adjusted engine response accordingly. The oil seals were changed to improve water and dust-proofing.

↑ **Lots of rocks but, fortunately, no roll. That Terrain Response System again is making light work of scrabbling over this uninviting outcrop. And check out the angle – Land Rovers seem to be able to defy gravity! (Nick Dimbleby)**

↑ One of the key elements of going off-road successfully is axle articulation – as can be seen here, the totally new design carried over the previous model's impressive performance in that direction. (Nick Dimbleby)

Transmission

The petrol engines were mated to a six-speed 'intelligent shift' electronically-controlled ZF 6HP26 automatic transmission, claimed to be one of the most advanced in the world. As well as 'normal' auto operation, it offered a 'sport' mode, which delivered more performance-oriented throttle response and gear shifts, and also had the Command Shift operation – which gave the driver full manual control of gear changing. In high range, it protected the engine by automatically changing up or down to prevent over-revving or stalling. In low range, this function was overridden to allow moving-off in a higher gear, so often useful in slippery conditions. And it got cleverer, because it was able electronically to analyse road conditions and the individual's own driving style, automatically tuning its responses accordingly. The particularly stiff case was unique to Land Rover, and had the gearbox electronic control unit housed within it, for extra protection. This communicated, via an electronic high-speed link, with the Terrain Response system.

The TDV6 was available either with the ZF auto 'box or a six-speed ZF manual gearbox. Enclosed in its unique casing, it had full compatibility with Terrain Response, and was aimed at the market in mainland Europe, where manual diesel vehicles dominated the 4x4 sector.

Drive, of course, went to all four wheels with Electronic Traction Control (ETC) and Dynamic Stability Control (DSC) to modulate power supply and braking, ensuring maximum grip in all conditions.

Throttle response, gear change patterns and suspension settings were also computer-controlled, according to speed and road (or off-road) conditions.

TRANSFER BOX AND DIFFERENTIALS

The two-speed transfer box featured an easy-to-use electronic shift, to move into low range (for off-road) or high range (for on-road), something which could be achieved on the move – a far cry from the clunky mechanical set-up of yore.

For added traction, the centre differential could be locked electronically when conditions required, enabling the vehicle to crawl, at low speed, over difficult terrain with more stability and less slip.

An electronically-controlled locking rear differential (known as an 'E-Diff') was also available with Terrain Response. All three differentials used in the Discovery 3 – forward, centre, and rear – were unique to the vehicle and mounted directly on to the chassis to maximise ground clearance for improved off-road agility.

TERRAIN RESPONSE SYSTEM

Terrain Response was previewed on the Range Stormer concept car and made its production debut on the Discovery 3. Standard on Discovery 3 models with air suspension, it was an advanced technology that optimised vehicle driveability and comfort, as well as maximising traction. The driver could simply select one of five Terrain Response settings to suit the driving conditions and a multitude of the vehicle's functions were tuned to deliver optimum performance. Accessed via a rotary control in the centre console, the five Terrain Response programs were; General Driving, Grass/Gravel/Snow, Mud and Ruts, Sand, Rock Crawl. The very clever electronics communicated with various other systems on the vehicle in order to produce the best results, thus:

Engine management system
The throttle map is altered, improving driveability by suiting torque delivery to the chosen terrain.

Electronic control system
Controls the automatic gearbox to optimise gear-change points.

Air suspension ride height
Automatically adjusts to give maximum height in the 'Rock Crawl' and 'Mud and Ruts' programs. This is also automatically activated whenever low range is selected.

Dynamic Stability Control (DSC)
Normally stops torque to a wheel after loss of traction, but in some off-road situations torque feed is still desirable, even when traction is being lost. Terrain Response automatically adjusts the DSC, so appropriate torque is maintained.

Electronic Traction Control, Brakeforce
Distribution and Anti-lock Brakes
These slip and braking control systems are all adjusted and tuned by Terrain Response to offer optimum grip, braking power, and safety on the chosen terrain.

Hill Descent Control (HDC)
The technology that automatically restricts speed downhill, using the anti-lock brakes, and enables drivers to remain in control even on the most slippery of downhill stretches. HDC is automatically engaged on all programs except 'general driving', and downhill speed rates vary depending on which surface is selected (in 'Rock Crawl' the lowest speed is selected to prevent vehicle damage).

Electronically-controlled centre and rear differentials
With different slip or locking rates for the different terrains.

The Terrain Response system works continuously, with the 'General Driving' program optimising the vehicle set-up for everyday on-road use. But, of course, it was the off-roading programs that demonstrated Land Rover's unique experience and expertise. 'We analysed the characteristics of nearly 50 different types of off-road surface, and

↓ Also impressive is the Discovery 3's cornering ability. Seen here testing on the test track at Land Rover's Gaydon HQ, the lack of body roll is apparent – you wouldn't want to corner at that speed in a Discovery 1! (Nick Dimbleby)

determined the vehicle system inputs necessary to optimise performance on each,' said chief programme engineer Steve Haywood. 'We concluded that these can be distilled into just a handful of programs – and those are the settings we offer on Terrain Response. It's like having an expert alongside you to help you get the best out of the vehicle, whatever the conditions, on-road or off.'

However you view it, this was some way from getting out to manually engage the front wheels on early Land Rovers!

Braking

All these clever technologies were linked to the standard four-channel ABS braking system. Two different braking specifications were offered,

depending on the vehicle, both providing large ventilated disc brakes all round (317mm x 30mm front discs and 325mm x 20mm rear discs) with twin-pot sliding callipers at the front and single-pot callipers at the rear. A more powerful braking system, used with the V8 engine, featured 337mm x 30mm front and 350mm x 20mm rear discs.

Electronic Brakeforce Distribution (EBD) provided optimal braking regardless of the way the vehicle was loaded, adjusting front-to-rear braking balance automatically. Emergency Brake Assist (EBA) automatically boosted pressure to the braking system if emergency braking was detected, reducing stopping distance and improving safety. For the first time on a Land Rover vehicle, the Discovery 3 featured an Electronic Park Brake, which was applied by a console-mounted switch and disengaged automatically when driving off.

↓ **Perhaps a little enthusiastic, but you can't blame Land Rover's test pilots for having fun once in a while! (Nick Dimbleby)**

Steering

Standard on all models was hydraulically-operated, power-assisted rack-and-pinion steering, designed to be both linear in feel and intuitive. The rack was mounted directly on to the frame to improve response and rigidity and was protected from rocks and other off-road snags by a substantial body-frame cross-member.

Suspension

As with any manufacturer of a large – and tall – 4x4, the suspension came in for serious scrutiny, the goal being to create a comfortable, on-road ride without compromising off-road ability. The

Discovery 3 was fitted with fully independent suspension and double wishbones front and rear. This was deemed to be an optimal set-up for on-road handling and refinement, despite offering some very impressive wheel travel figures – 255mm at the front and 330mm at the rear – for excellent wheel articulation and off-road traction. Coil-spring suspension with hydraulic dampers was standard on entry-level models, but all higher-specification Discovery 3 models featured cross-linked air suspension, increasing on-road refinement, off-road capability, and overall versatility.

The air springs were computer-controlled, giving softer or firmer springing automatically, depending on road or track conditions. Being cross-linked further aided off-road capability, special software detecting off-road driving and cross-connecting the system. Air

↑ It might not climb every mountain, but it'll give most of them a run for their money! And it goes without saying … (Nick Dimbleby)

displaced by the upward movement of an air spring is transferred to the spring on the opposite side, forcing it down, improving composure. In essence, this mimics the action of a traditional beam axle, by boosting articulation and improving wheel contact.

The air springs also provided a range of ride heights which improved access to the vehicle, by selecting the 'low' height setting, and giving extra ground clearance when off-roading by selecting the 'high' setting. The height setting could be selected manually or automatically by the Terrain Response system.

The multi-purpose tyres were specially developed for the Discovery 3 and could handle some light off-roading as well as on-road use. All wheels were alloys, in sizes from 17in (235/70 tyres), through the most popular 18in (255/60 tyres) to the very 'bling' 19in (255/55 tyres).

↑ ... that only Hippos are more at home in deep, thick, power-sapping mud. At one time, the driver would have to spend some while selecting exactly the right drive/diff combination; with TRS, it's just a click away. (Nick Dimbleby)

Testing

Of course, all the grand plans and theoretical designs are as nothing if the finished article can't come up with the goods. With impressive 4 x 4 opposition from Europe, in the shape of BMW and VW/Porsche, and the usual Japanese suspects, the Discovery 3 had a heavy burden to carry. So it was put through the wringer during an incredible four-million-mile test programme. The punishing regime

took place on five continents, on-road, off-road, and just about everything in between. According to chief programme engineer, Steve Haywood, 'We believe few, if any, vehicles have ever undergone a more punishing and varied series of tests.'

Off-road testing

Land Rover's off-road testing schedule is arguably the most demanding of any vehicle manufacturer. The Discovery 3 had to be able to wade in water 700mm deep, climb and descend 45° gradients, remain stable when driving across a 35° slope, and operate in temperatures ranging from -40°C to +50°C. Oh, and the handbrake had to be capable of holding the vehicle on a 45° slope.

Much of the fundamental work (wading, slippery grass, deep mud, etc.) was undertaken at Eastnor Castle (in Herefordshire) and private estates in Scotland. Durability testing was carried out on army test tracks at Bagshot in Surrey, and Bovington in Dorset, facilities normally used for destruction-testing tanks. The new Integrated Body-frame and suspension had a real work-out there!

Similar testing was carried out at a former military facility in South Africa, a country also used for hot weather and dust testing, as was Australia, where vast distances were covered in the outback, including testing on vicious corrugated roads.

Dubai was the venue for evaluating the vehicle's ability to climb sand dunes, and for general off-road ability. The new and advanced air-conditioning system also had to prove its worth in the extreme heat. Performance testing in ice and snow was carried out in northern Canada and Sweden, where temperatures were regularly as low as minus 40°C.

On-road testing

Unusually, on-road trials involved a large amount of time spent at places normally associated with sports cars, including high-speed testing at the famous original Nürburgring circuit in Germany, where on-road handling and braking performance were pushed to the limit. At the Nardo bowl in southern Italy, Discovery 3 test vehicles lapped continuously for 20 hours a day at, or near, maximum speed. The 12-week programme involved 31,000 miles of maximum speed driving.

On-road composure was tuned at the Millbrook proving ground in Bedfordshire, the MIRA test track in Warwickshire, and at Ford's Lommel engineering facility in Belgium, which included the notorious Belgian pavé.

Tokyo was the venue for city-driving tests, including its ability in stop-start traffic and the efficacy of the air-conditioning system. Traffic testing was also carried out in oven-hot Las Vegas, high-altitude Denver, and in New York, where radio reception and navigation were checked out among the giant man-made canyons.

A natural towing vehicle, test cars were regularly seen to be dashing up and down Austrian mountain passes with a 3.5 tonne trailer on the back.

Awards

So, after all that design, development, testing and, let's be honest, PR hype, did the Discovery 3 come up with the goods? Well, if Land Rover's burgeoning trophy cabinet is anything to go by, yes is the answer; by the beginning of 2008, the Discovery 3 had

won over 100 international awards – a record for any SUV – and they came from all over the world, including Russia and China.

To list them all would take up too much space, but here's a representative sample:

In February 2006, the Discovery collected the AXA Car of the Year 2006 awards in Northern Ireland. The title was awarded by the Ulster Motoring Writers Association (UMWA) who chose the Discovery 3 as the winner of the AXA Leisure Car category before being crowned the AXA Car of the Year 2006, beating tough competition from Lexus, Audi, and Toyota. Chairman of the UMWA, Jim McCauley, said: 'Of all the vehicles judged in this year's competition the Discovery 3 scored consistently high. It scooped almost twice the number of points of its nearest rival, which really sets it apart in its class. As well as its on-and-off-road capability, it offers a quality driving experience and is an outstanding testament to the UK motor industry.'

In January 2007, *What Car?* magazine named the Discovery 3 TDV6 SE auto the Best Large 4 × 4 for the third year running – i.e. for every full year of its production, it took the title!

↑ **A Discovery without towing ability would have been unthinkable. The Discovery 3 (seen here with another design classic in the shape of an American Airstream trailer) regularly carted off 'best tow car' awards.**

And in June 2007, the Discovery 3 completed another 'double triple' by winning the *Auto Express* Best 4x4 Off-Roader category, beating the Mercedes M-Class and BMW X5 in the process. Land Rover's managing director, Phil Popham, said: 'Achieving the Best 4 x 4 Off-Roader award for the Discovery 3 – a car that continues to be an outstanding success, consistently beating new entrants from other manufacturers – is a testament to its class-leading diesel engine, its versatility, and its all-round package.'

The Discovery 3 was designed with towing in mind, and the effort that went into its towing abilities was rewarded at the 2007 inaugural *Practical Caravan, What Car?* and the Camping & Caravanning Club Towcar awards. There it took the silverware for the Best Towcar over 1,900kg. Judges rated the Discovery 3's exceptional capability, saying: 'The Discovery 3 will happily tow at 60mph all day, and smoothes away bumps that are felt with a thump in many other 4x4s. Nothing else in this class is as accomplished an all-rounder; it's great to drive solo, tows with gusto, and is supremely practical.'

Planet 4x4 magazine, in October 2007, named the Discovery 3 as the Most Practical 4x4. In the first assessment of its kind, it scored an impressive 93 points out of a 100, ahead of the Mercedes GL, Audi Q7, Nissan Pathfinder, and Lexus RX. Editor Alan Kidd added: 'This is probably the most intense scrutiny a group of 4x4s has ever been put under. Our testers crawled all over each of the 38 vehicles, examining every last detail of what makes a car easy to live with. There are some incredibly clever packaging solutions out there – but nothing to beat the Discovery 3. From its handy double glovebox to its brilliant seat-folding system, it sets the standard for load carrying and does a proper job of taking seven fully grown adults. It's a perfectly executed example of how a vehicle's interior should be, and richly deserves the title of Britain's Most Practical 4x4.' At the end of the year, *Planet 4x4* went the whole hog and voted the Discovery 3 as the Best 4x4 on the Planet! The only obvious drawback here is that it's hard to see how it could be bettered. Fighting off competition from 36 other vehicles, it proved unbeatable on practicality, packaging, off-road ability, and all-round dynamics, scoring 819.4 out of a possible 1,000. To add to Land Rover's joy, the Range Rover was runner-up, with the Range Rover Sport and Freelander 2 clocking up class wins.

G4 Challenge – The return of The Camel

From 1980, the off-roading world revelled in the real-life, Boys' Own adventures of competitors in the Camel Trophy and were quite rightly disappointed when it ceased in 2000 (see Chapter 8). However, in 2003 Land Rover instituted the G4 Challenge which effectively replaced the Camel Trophy and, likewise, was a serious test of men and machines. Each team of two people was confronted with a test of physical and mental agility, not to mention some serious skill when it came to driving off-road – in a Land Rover vehicle of course.

The four stages took part in different time zones: 2003 – USA, Canada, South Africa, and Australia (winner Rudi Thoelen, Belgium); 2006 – Thailand, Laos, Brazil, and Bolivia (winner Martin Dreyer, South-Africa). For 2003, the showcased vehicle was the Discovery II, but in 2006 it was the Discovery 3 which took centre stage – 39 were prepared, with 38 being used.

Despite the arduous nature of the event, the vehicles were not modified, the only changes being bolt-on accessories (roof racks, winches, snorkel, protective guards, ancillary lighting, etc.) and the vivid Tangiers Orange paint finish, making them unmissable.

The 2008/09 Challenge was in the planning stage at the time of writing, and was being staged to support the International Federation of Red Cross and Red Crescent Societies which is the world's largest humanitarian organisation, providing assistance without discrimination to around 233 million people every year. Land Rover expected to generate over £1m during the course of the next two Land Rover G4 Challenge cycles. As ever, the selection process itself was gruelling. This was to ensure that entrants would be able to cope with such activities as mountain biking, kayaking, climbing, orienteering, and abseiling. As well tests of driving skill, initiative, and strategic thinking, teams were also competing against each other in physical fitness. For the first time, each of the 18 teams from around the world would consist of one male and one female entrant. The victorious team will present a Land Rover to the National Society

↑ For the ultimate in off-roading, the G4 Challenge replaced the much-lamented Camel Trophy and was just as tough on both man (and from 2008, woman) and machine. The new car first featured in 2006 ... (Nick Dimbleby)

in their country. Predictably, the environment is carefully considered and the Challenge had its carbon dioxide offset through Climate Care. Throughout all stages of the event, an environmental consultant was on board to ensure best practice.

As with the Camel Trophy, the G4 vehicles had to be disposed of after the event. Some went to the crusher, but many are now in the hands of private owners, most of whom are members of the G4 Owners Club, formed early in 2007.

In persuit of perfection

Land Rover loves its special editions, so the Discovery Pursuit was no real surprise.

Launched in March 2007, only 300 were made, all of which were based on the TDV6 GS model, with Java Black paintwork, Ebony interior, 19in alloy wheels, body-coloured wheelarch surrounds, manual operation leather seats, automatic transmission and chrome-finish mirror caps. The on-the-road price of £30,995 included a carbon offset for the first 45,000 miles (see below).

→ (overleaf) ... and unsurprisingly rose to the challenge with aplomb, carrying huge loads of men and equipment across the most unpleasant terrain, from harsh, hard-baking deserts, to muddy river crossings. (Nick Dimbleby)

Carbon offset

Regardless of how well new technology has been applied to the Discovery 3 (and other Land Rover products), it is a big, heavy vehicle and, though relatively economical, in real terms it was always going to bend the plastic at fill-up time. Making it achieve, say, 40mpg was never viable, but Land Rover approached the problem of climate change and pollution from another direction, by introducing a comprehensive carbon offset programme.

This was achieved by offsetting CO_2 emissions at its two production facilities and implementing a UK customer programme to offset the first 45,000 miles of vehicle use. This unique initiative was managed by Climate Care, an award-winning organisation which puts funds towards sustainable energy projects.

CO2 OFFSETS IN DETAIL

CO_2 is a greenhouse gas that is released when fossil fuels such as oil, gas, and coal are burnt. By offsetting, the purchaser is, in effect, paying someone to reduce CO_2 in the atmosphere on your behalf. The funds raised help to create a lower-carbon world.

NEW VEHICLE OFFSETS

This programme offsets the CO_2 emissions from the manufacture of all Land Rovers and the first 45,000 miles used by vehicles sold in the UK. Customers receive a vehicle window sticker and a certificate from Climate Care confirming participation.

The cost of this offset cover is included in the purchase price of the vehicle. This scheme invests in a specific range of Land Rover-funded CO_2-reduction projects around the world. All of the projects funded through this scheme go through a rigorous process of verification and validation to ensure and demonstrate the CO_2 emissions saved.

EXISTING VEHICLE OFFSETS

Owners of vehicles sold before the introduction of the new vehicle programme, or for whom the original offset mileage is exceeded, can purchase offsets directly through a dedicated Land Rover calculator, administered by Climate Care. Customers will receive a vehicle window sticker and a certificate from Climate Care confirming participation. This incorporates elements of the new vehicle scheme, but invests in Climate Care's general portfolio of renewable energy, energy efficiency and technology change projects.

The 2007 model year

If it ain't broke, don't fix it – wise words heeded by Land Rover who simply tweaked the Discovery 3 in October 2006 (for the 2007 model year). A small improvement in fuel consumption and reduction in CO_2 emissions meant that the TDV6 range achieved full EU4 emissions compliance. Reversing sensors were added to the entry level seven-seater TDV6 (GS), and for the first time an electronic onboard Tyre Pressure Monitoring System was an option (at £385). The Premium navigation system had the option of hybrid television, capable of receiving both analogue and digital TV signals, priced at £500. Other minor improvements were the introduction of the one-touch opening passenger window and the 'destination input on the move' function for the navigation system.

However, the most important option offered was the Land Rover Watch stolen vehicle tracking device, increasingly important as car thieves moved more

towards burgling homes for car keys to steal vehicles, or worse, car-jacking the vehicle from the owner. This method, of course, meant that there was no need to overcome complex alarm and immobiliser systems. Figures at the time suggested that over 50% of stolen vehicles were never recovered.

With Land Rover Watch, the vehicle could be tracked across Europe using GSM (phone) and GPS technology. And, with its Thatcham Category 5 approval, there was the possibility of some insurance discount to offset the £999 cost.

The line-up and prices for the 2007 model year were as follows:

TDV6 five-seater	£27,215
TDV6 GS	£29,715
TDV6 XS	£32,715
TDV6 SE	£37,215
TDV6 HSE	£43,715

↓ **The 2007 model year brought some nice tweaks, but the major talking point was the optional Land Rover Watch, a Thatcham-approved vehicle tracking system, rapidly becoming an essential accessory. (Land Rover)**

Commercially speaking

On 19 March 2007, the Discovery 3 Commercial went on sale. It was engineered with approval from HM Revenue and Customs (HMRC) in order to gain N1 Light Commercial 4 x 4 Vehicle status – good news for business users who were able to take advantage of the benefit-in-kind tax and full VAT reclaim associated with Light Commercial Vehicles. Two models were available; the base model and the better-equipped XS version. Along with 2,130 litres of load space, each came with a full-length phenolic floor, privacy glass, two-piece bulkhead, four-corner air suspension and Terrain Response. Like all other current Land Rover vehicles, they also included a CO_2 offset for the first 45,000 miles within the on-the-road price.

↑ **All that low-down diesel torque allied to loads of loadspace and superb towing ability meant that, like its immediate predecessor, a commercial (rear-windowless) version just had to happen. (Land Rover)**

The complete specifications were as follows:

DISCOVERY 3 COMMERCIAL

17in alloy wheels, four-corner air suspension, privacy glass, and window inserts, non-smokers pack, Four-Channel all-terrain ABS, central high-mounted stop lamp, Active Roll Mitigation, cloth seats, full length phenolic load space floor, manual six-speed transmission, volumetric alarm, Noble Plate Finish, Electronic Brake Assist, Dynamic Stability Control, electronic park brake, two-piece bulkhead.

DISCOVERY 3 XS COMMERCIAL

As standard Commercial plus powerfold exterior mirrors, roof rails, 18in alloy wheels, cruise control, bright pack, heated front screen and washer jets, rear park distance control, Hi ICE pack, Air Con ATC.

VEHICLE TECH SPEC

	Discovery 3 Commercial	Discovery 3 XS Commercial
Price	£28,240	£31,740
Load space		
Load space volume (litres)	2130	2130
Weights		
EEC kerb weight (kg)	2593 (max)	2602 (max)
Max front axle (kg)	1450	1450
Max rear axle (kg)	1855	1855
Fuel economy		
Urban mpg (man/auto)	25.4/21.6	25.4/21.6
Extra urban mpg (man/auto)	34.9/33.2	34.9/33.2
Combined mpg (man/auto)	30.7/27.7	30.7/27.7
CO_2 – g/km (man/auto)	244/270	244/270
Towing		
Max towing (kg)	3500	3500

Four million – and counting!

8 May 2007 was a historic date for the Land Rover company because on that day it produced its four millionth vehicle. Suitably, for us at least, it was a Discovery 3 which was donated to the Born Free Foundation, an international charity dedicated to wildlife conservation and animal welfare. It was collected by the actress Joanna Lumley, a patron of Born Free, and became a Rapid Response Rescue vehicle for deployment across the UK and Europe.

Taking the highway

The UK Highways Agency, responsible for maintaining and operating England's motorways and major A-roads, needed a fleet of large, capable, and reliable vehicles, up to the task of operating in a wide variety of road – and off-road – conditions. And they don't have to be shy of hard work, with each vehicle typically clocking over 200,000 miles in 18 months. Not surprisingly, when it came to renewing its existing Land Rover line-up, they were replaced by 49 Discovery 3s. These arrived just in time to be put to good use during the dreadful floods of 2007.

4 MILLIONTH LAND ROVER
8th MAY 2007
LAND ROVER
BORN FREE FOUNDATION
Donated To The Born Free Foundation

← On 8 May 2007 Land Rover produced its four millionth vehicle, an Absolutely Fabulous Discovery 3. Donated to the wildlife conservation and animal welfare Born Free Foundation, it was collected by patron Joanna Lumley. (Land Rover)

← In 2007 the Highways Agency replaced existing Land Rovers with Discovery 3s. Its all-round abilities were the main reason for the move and they were invaluable in the heavy flooding of that year. (Land Rover)

The 2008 model year

Discovery 3 improvements for 2008 were aimed mainly at the cabin area to give occupants a higher level of luxury – though this was hardly an unpleasant place to be to start with.

For the first time, real wood veneer finish (Straight Grained Walnut or Grand Black Lacquer) was available on HSE models, as were premium ruched leather seats, driver's seat cushion pocket, eight-way passenger seat adjustment, premium carpet mats and, in some markets, an electrically-adjustable steering column and driver's seat powered lumbar support. Further upgrades across the model range included a more premium Ebony centre stack and centre floor console, Noble Plate Finish to facia air vents and other controls, and silver-plated finish to the speaker bezels.

Due to the overwhelming demand for the efficient Discovery 3 TDV6 (and the 32 per cent more economical Range Rover and Range Rover Sport TDV8 models), the sale of naturally-aspirated petrol models ceased from the 2008 model year. This meant that Land Rover's UK diesel sales looked set to exceed 90 per cent of the total that year.

By February 2008, the Discovery 3 specification and options list had become almost an industry in itself, with what seemed innumerable combinations on offer for the well-heeled purchaser.

OPTION PACKS

SEVEN SEAT PACK	TDV6				
	5 seat	GS	XS	SE	HSE
7 seats (including 3rd row head airbag)	N/A	S	S	S	S
Accessory socket row 3/load space	N/A	S	S	S	S
Complex 35:30:35 2nd row seat	N/A	S	S	S	S
Map lamps row 3	N/A	S	S	S	S

BRIGHT PACK	TDV6				
	5 seat	GS	XS	SE	HSE
Front fog lamps	N/A	O	S	S	S
Automatic headlights	N/A	O	S	S	S
Rain sensor	N/A	O	S	S	S
Electrochromic interior mirror	N/A	O	S	S	S
Puddle and footwell lamps	N/A	O	S	S	S
Headlamp powerwash	N/A	O	S	S	S

CONVENIENCE PACK	TDV6				
	5 seat	GS	XS	SE	HSE
Complex 35:30:35 row 2 seat	O	N/A	S	S	S
Illuminated vanity mirrors	O	N/A	S	S	S
Rear luggage net	O	N/A	S	S	S
Third cupholder row 1	O	N/A	S	S	S

LEATHER PACK	TDV6				
	5 seat	GS	XS	SE	HSE
Leather gear knob and gaiter	N/A	N/A	N/A	S	N/A
Leather seats (powered and driver's armrest)	N/A	N/A	N/A	S	N/A
Driver memory pack – driver seat/ mirrors	N/A	N/A	N/A	S	N/A
Electrically-adjustable steering column	N/A	N/A	N/A	S	N/A

PREMIUM LEATHER PACK	TDV6				
	5 seat	GS	XS	SE	HSE
Premium leather seats, leather gear knob, and gaiter	N/A	N/A	N/A	N/A	S
Eight-way electrically-powered driver and passenger seats	N/A	N/A	N/A	N/A	S
Driver's seat memory, driver's seat powered lumber support, driver's seat cushion pocket	N/A	N/A	N/A	N/A	S
Electrically-adjustable steering column	N/A	N/A	N/A	N/A	S

HI ICE PACK	TDV6				
	5 seat	GS	XS	SE	HSE
Harman/Kardon audio, 8 speakers, passive subwoofer, audio amplifier, steering wheel mounted audio controls	N/A	N/A	S	N/A	N/A
Six-disc in-dash CD player	N/A	N/A	S	N/A	N/A

PREMIUM ICE PACK	TDV6				
	5 seat	GS	XS	SE	HSE
Harman/Kardon Logic 7 audio system, 13 speakers, active subwoofer, DSP amplifier, remote audio controls	N/A	N/A	N/A	S	S
Six-disc in-dash CD player	N/A	N/A	S	S	S

TOW PACK	TDV6				
	5 seat	GS	XS	SE	HSE
Plug-in tow ball	O	O	O	O	O

Key: S = Standard, O = Optional,
NCO = No cost option,
N/A = Not applicable

INTERIOR AND EXTERIOR COLOUR COMBINATIONS

EXTERIOR	INTERIOR		
	Tundra	Ebony	Alpaca
Alaska White	R	R	A
Atacama Sand	A	R	D
Buckingham Blue	A	R	R
Cairns Blue	*	A	R
Izmir Blue	*	R	R
Java Black	A	R	D
Keswick Green	R	R	*
Lugano Teal	*	R	R
Rimini Red	A	D	D
Stornoway Grey	R	D	D
Tonga Green	D	A	D
Vienna Green	D	R	A
Zermatt Silver	R	D	R

D Designer's choice   A Combination is available
R Recommended choice   * Combination is not available

The shape of things to come

Land Rover's LRX diesel concept vehicle made its European debut in Geneva at the 78e Salon International de l'Auto (6-16 March 2008), and clearly showed the way the company was heading. The vehicle itself was not in the same size class as the Discovery, being both lower and shorter even than the existing Freelander. Nevertheless, advances in vehicle production methods and weight-saving techniques would be applied to all vehicles. And its engine was of great interest, being a highly fuel-efficient 2.0-litre turbo diesel hybrid. In combination with other Land Rover technologies, this powertrain could reduce fuel consumption by as much as 30% compared to other 4 x 4s of comparable size. And it incorporated an Electric Rear Axle Drive (ERAD) which enabled the LRX to use electric drive alone at lower speeds, while retaining full (even improved) 4 x 4 ability in tough conditions. Doubtless, it gives us a few clues as to how the Discovery 4 might be produced.

↓ **The shape of Land Rovers to come? Hard to believe now, but pondering the Discovery 3 at the time of the original launch in 1989 would have been just as incredible as the 2008 LRX concept vehicle. (Land Rover)**

CHAPTER 5
LET'S OFF-ROAD!

Despite its school-run, tarmac-trekking image, the Discovery is a mightily competent off-road tool; and why not, as its basic chassis, suspension, and drivetrain layout is essentially the same as the Classic Range Rover and Defender.

There's no doubt that off-roading is a whole load of fun and, compared with most other forms of motor 'sport', extremely safe. As has often been said, it's a great adrenaline rush at just 2mph! However, the technique of driving without tarmac under the wheels is absolutely nothing like normal driving, and to a great extent you have to unlearn everything you've ever learned. You are heartily recommended to try at least one day at a specialist training course, where you can learn the new skills required to be safe off-road.

You can go off-roading with Land Rover itself, at one of its four sites, or with one of the many other off-road centres. The photographs in this chapter were taken at one of David Mitchell's Landcraft days, set in the staggering scenery of Snowdonia National Park and offering terrain of just about every hue. Like many such centres, you can choose between specific training sessions or just turning up and enjoying yourself on the huge off-road area. My thanks to David and Landcraft marshal, Dylan Williams, for their help.

Note that this chapter can only cover the basic rules of driving off-road. For an in-depth study, consult Jack Jackson's Haynes publication, *The Off-Road 4-Wheel-Drive Book*.

Where to get off-road

Despite the government's best efforts (aided and abetted by many pressure groups, some with rather dubious motives), there are still plenty of green lanes suitable for legal off-roading. However, it is vital that you check and double-check that the lanes you use are specified for your use – you cannot afford to give ammunition to the we-want-the-countryside-for-ourselves brigade. You'll need the very latest, large-scale Ordnance Survey maps, but even they need checking-up on as changes made to lanes can take some years to appear in print. By far the best way to approach the subject is to join a local club – either a general 4x4 club or one specifically for Discoverys and/or Land Rovers. Most have officers who deal with green-laning issues and keep in touch with the councils to keep tabs on which lanes are officially open to vehicles and which aren't. It also gives you the opportunity to take part in an organised drive which not only adds a pleasant social element to the day, but also means that there's someone to help out should you get it all wrong.

All the photographs in this book which show vehicles off-road were taken either on official off-road routes, at purpose-made off-road centres, or on private land with the owners' permission.

Preparation

The Discovery is more or less ready to go, with tyres (see below) being probably the most important factor. For standard green-laning or a reasonable off-road course, you won't need to do anything much to your car. However, remember that extras such as side steps and a towing bracket will limit your ground clearance, and of course the front spoiler (with its lights) is also directly in the firing line. It's the driver that needs the most preparation and it's advisable to take at least some off-road training before you

← Don't look down – an American Discovery 3-wheels down a vertiginous track. (Nick Dimbleby)

> **DID YOU KNOW?**
> No matter how gentle the off-road manoeuvre, remember that you should always keep your thumbs on the outside of the steering wheel. If you don't and there's a sudden kickback – say where a tyre drops into a rut or hits a large obstacle – the rapid spinning of the steering wheel could break your fifth digits!

venture out solo. Remember that green lanes are public roads and that you and your passengers should wear seat belts at all times. Even on a private site, this is an essential safety measure – imagine up-ending your Discovery *without* seat belts!

It is definitely *not* recommended to go off-roading alone for obvious safety reasons. Always take a first-aid kit with you, and a 12v tyre-inflator is useful, as it means you can lower the tyre pressures when required, knowing they can be returned to the original figures when driving home. CB radio or two-way walkie-talkies are handy tools to have. Carry something in the way of sustenance (a Thermos with a hot drink, sandwiches, chocolate, etc) and always make sure you've a full tank of fuel before you start – remember that off-roading can reduce your typical mpg by 50 per cent or even more. Empty the car of non-essential contents and tie everything down that's likely to fly around as the car goes over very uneven surfaces and up steep inclines.

When you come back onto metalled roads, be aware that lots of mud and grit in the wheels, steering, and brakes will do them no good at all. Make sure they work efficiently and take the first opportunity you can to blast them clean. It's a good

↑ → **Clambering up a rocky, rutted track, having passed several struggling mountain goats on the way, and with a deep breath … it's down the other side – no time to get vertigo.**

↑ Check out that massive axle articulation – it's what other 4x4s can only dream of. (Nick Dimbleby)

→ An early three-door complete with non-too subtle graphics sits atop a Welsh mountain – and not a school in sight! Note the massive off-road tyres fitted to this particular car.

↑ Water, water everywhere, and enthusiastic Discovery owners can't resist it. All that traction and ground clearance make gullies such as this a breeze. However, it's vital to make sure what lies under the water before you pile in – it's no fun to get half way and realise that there's a huge hole or large rock just below the surface.

→ Further on in the Landcraft site there's a lovely mixture of sudden steep incline, stone surface made extra slippery by the small stream, large jagged rocks at the top making it essential to get exactly the right line (something further complicated by the tree on the right of the photo) and, of course, an absolute mud-bath just before the top. Well, life has to have a challenge!

→ Even better than some water to splash around in is a great deep quagmire to really test your skills; blend subtle throttle control with the right gear and the courage of your convictions and it's easy. Remember that this is a special site, designed specially for this kind of treatment; doing this on public lanes is definitely not the thing to do.

↓ The Discovery was designed for off-roading and is very competent even in standard form. However, for competition (or just plain fun!) you can go to extremes, as with this serious piece of off-road kit, seen at the McDonald Landrover workshop.

→ **A range of off-road driving courses and competitions are run around the country to help hone your skills.** (Nick Dimbleby)

reason to buy a pressure washer, because no garage forecourt will want you using theirs and clogging up the drains with half a tonne of mud!

Clearance

Make sure you understand and know exactly what your vehicle is capable of. Regardless of your school maths results, there are three angles that you need to know, as follows:

• The approach angle is that between your car and an incline. You need to make sure that your front wheels touch the hill before your front spoiler.

• The ramp angle defines the side steepness of a hill – you don't want to get your Discovery beached on its belly.

• The departure angle is the opposite of the approach angle and relates to the angle of the hill in relation to the lower rear of the vehicle. The Discovery is good in this area, though a towing bracket seriously inhibits its performance.

Get any of these wrong and you could not only damage the vehicle but also put yourself (and your passengers) in danger.

Tyres

All the traction in the world is useless if you have no grip, and that's the job of the tyres. Most Discoverys leave the factory with road-biased tyres fitted, which are usually described as being an 80/20 balance in favour of metalled roads. They'll offer almost saloon car levels of comfort, grip, and quiet and be quite capable when dealing with minor off-road excursions. At the other extreme, there's the MT (mud-terrain) type of tyre, which has tread deep enough to swallow small children whole and which will grip in mud and snow like no road tyre. These are designed to clear away the mud as if it wasn't there, and though they can be used on metalled

roads, they will compromise cornering and handling and cabin noise levels will increase dramatically. In common with many enthusiasts, the author lives in a part of the country where bad winter weather is a foregone conclusion – namely above the snow line in the Cambrian mountains. The answer here was to buy a set of cheap, steel wheels and use them as 'slaves' for a set of serious MT rubber for use from November–March. At that point, the standard alloys can be replaced along with the 'road' tyres. Clearly, this is also a principle that applies if you intend going to off-road days or courses – it takes half an hour or less to change them, so it's not as if it's hard work.

Make sure, however, that you only use road-legal tyres if you're going off-road down official green lanes. Firstly, these lanes are still classed as public highways so you'd be running illegally with non-road tyres. Secondly, these would churn up the ground in no uncertain fashion, which is something nobody wants.

Gearing down

All Discoverys have low-range gearing and by using that little gear lever in front of the main one, you can

↑ **There's a huge difference between proper off-road tyres and mainly-motorway rubber. At left is a Goodyear MT (mud-terrain) Wrangler, with very deep tread. The Goodyear Eagle GT+4 on the right, has been constructed with tarmac in mind and offers extra on-road cornering and braking, better mileage, and better mpg.**

→ **So that's what that extra gear lever is for! Push forward to get a set of lower gear ratios ideal for off-roading. All Series 1 Discoverys (and the 2003 Series 2 model) had a manually-engaged differential lock which made it possible to get through seemingly impenetrable mud and up incredibly steep inclines.**

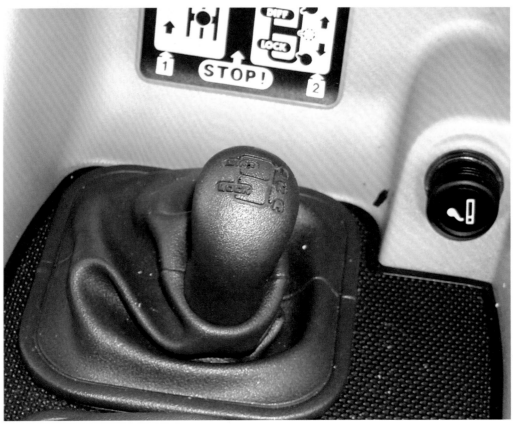

enter those low ratios – known by most as low box. The gearing is reduced by a ratio of 2:1, and it's this that makes the Discovery so useful off-road, allowing the car to travel very slowly without the need to use the clutch or brakes, which is ideal for coming down steep, muddy hills where using either would result in a very unpleasant scene indeed. The Series 2 Discovery can use a unique hill descent control. Once activated, this HDC will use the ABS brakes to keep the vehicle at a constant low speed. The system works when first and reverse gears are selected.

Land Rover's TREAD lightly policy

Land Rover itself recommends a policy of TREAD lightly, where the word is a mnemonic listing the essential points of safe and considerate off-road driving, viz:

T: TRAVEL ONLY WHERE PERMITTED

Travel only on trails, roads, or land areas that are open to vehicles or other forms of travel. Make sure the trail you plan to use is available for your type of vehicle. Wide vehicles on narrow trails can damage both the trail and your vehicle. Cutting switchbacks or taking shortcuts can destroy vegetation and cause others to use the unauthorised route. Most trails and routes designated for 4x4 use are constructed to withstand the effects of use. Staying on these trails reduces the impact of 4x4 vehicles.

R: RESPECT THE RIGHTS OF OTHERS

Respect and be courteous to other users who also want to enjoy the land you are using. Be considerate and honour their desire for solitude and a peaceful countryside experience. Loud motors and noisy behaviour are not acceptable and detract from a quiet outdoor setting. Give other people the space and quiet you would appreciate.

Driving near or around someone's camp site is not appreciated. When driving, be especially cautious around horses or hikers. Pull off to the side of the track, shut off your engine, and allow the horses or hikers to pass.

In and around campsites, be sensitive to campers' need for a peaceful atmosphere. If your exhaust silencer is not quiet, push your machine into and out of a campsite, with the engine shut off.

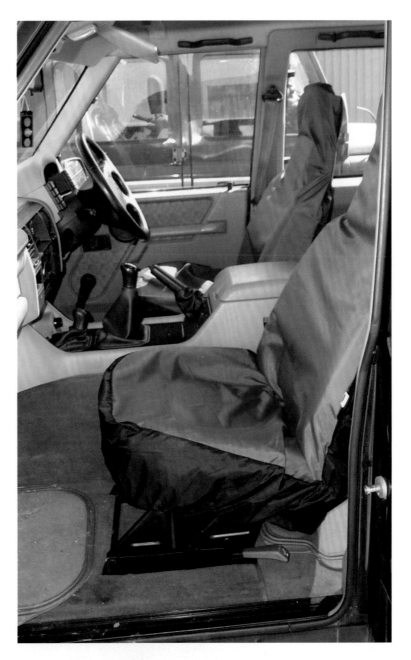

E: EDUCATE YOURSELF

Educate yourself by dropping in and talking with land managers at their offices. Or, if you see them in the field, stop and ask questions. They can tell you what areas and routes are suitable for off-roading. Travel maps are usually available at most offices. On private lands, be sure to obtain the owner or land manager's permission to cross or use their lands. As you travel the countryside, comply with trail and road signs. Honour all gates, fences, and barriers that are there to protect the natural resources, wildlife and livestock – and ultimately, our right to drive off-road.

↑ Another cheap but very worthwhile investment is a set of wipe-clean, protective seat covers. They're essential for off-roading days and handy for use during the dirty winter months.

→ **Edging carefully down a really rocky outcrop with a brave colleague making sure nothing grounds out.** (Nick Dimbleby)

↑ A serious off-road-
racing modified Discovery
makes a splash.
(Nick Dimbleby)

A: AVOID STREAMS, MEADOWS, AND WILDLIFE

Avoid sensitive areas at all times. In early spring and autumn, rain and snow typically saturate the ground making soil surfaces soft. Improper vehicle use can cause damage to vegetation and ground surface. Stay on designated roadways and trails so that new scars are not established. Especially sensitive areas susceptible to scarring are stream banks, lake shores, and meadows. Cross streams only at fords where the road or trail intersects the stream. Travelling in a stream channel is unacceptable and causes damage to aquatic life. Hillside climbing may be a challenge, but once vehicle scars are established, other vehicles follow the same ruts and do long-lasting damage. Rain causes further damage by washing deep gullies in tyre ruts. Permanent and unsightly scars result. While operating your 4x4, be sensitive to the life-sustaining needs of wildlife and livestock. In deep snow, stay clear of wildlife, so that vehicle noise and close proximity does not increase stress on animals and birds struggling to survive.

D: DRIVE AND TRAVEL RESPONSIBLY

Drive and travel responsibly to protect the forests, lands, and waters that you enjoy. You enjoy the outdoors for a number of good reasons – the countryside is beautiful; you have freedom to roam vast scenic areas; you see clear flowing streams and rivers; you see wild animals and birds; you breathe clean air; you see and smell fragrant and colourful vegetation, trees, flowers and brush; you develop a sense of being a part of this great and expansive outdoors!

These and others are reasons enough for you to do all you can to help protect the lands that mean so much to you. There are places to practise for the G4 Challenge, but they don't include green lanes!

Help preserve the beauty and the inspiring attributes of our countryside for yourself and new generations to follow.

↓ It's not all slow-speed manoeuvering – Discoverys are raced on a regular basis. (Nick Dimbleby)

CHAPTER 6
CHOOSING & BUYING A DISCOVERY

The Club connection

So, you're convinced that the Discovery is for you? The first thing to realise is that over half a million have left the production line since it first appeared in 1989, so there's no shortage of choice and no reason to rush out and buy a bad one. As with most cars, membership of the owners club is a good starting place. The Discovery Owners Club is a repository of information, and often club members are selling their own cars – by definition, these tend to be better looked-after than most. It's also a place to meet owners of like mind and to buy used parts and accessories. Check Appendix A for details.

Where to buy

A new Discovery? Well lucky old you! Apart from finding a wheelbarrow large enough to take all that cash, buying a new Discovery isn't at all difficult. However, there's currently lots of dissent among the UK car-buying public, who have realised that in many cases a British-built car can be purchased much cheaper on mainland Europe. We're talking many thousands of pounds here, so it might be worth your while investigating this option. Always make sure that the car you buy has full UK specification with a mph speedometer, headlamps that dip to the left, etc. If you don't fancy the hassle and paperwork, a number of 'personal import' companies exist and will sell to the UK buyer hassle-free. Clearly, the saving is less, but usually still considerable.

At the time of writing buying a used Discovery 3 almost always means a trip to a Land Rover franchised dealer. Over the years, the company has pushed its image and showrooms gradually upmarket, to the point where only young cars can be found on their forecourts. Because of this, and the insistence on relatively low mileages, Land Rover dealerships

can offer impressive and comprehensive warranties, which is a very big plus on something as complex as a Discovery 3 – just imagine the cost when one or two of those clever black boxes need replacing! Buying a recent Series 3 or late Series 2 privately is a bit of a lottery; obviously, being just a few years old, the car should be OK, but why is the owner selling it? And why not just trade it in? You are well-advised to take an expert with you again, largely because of all those complex electronic systems. Take great care that the car in question has not been stolen or ringed (see further on).

If you're buying a very early model, look out for the press and factory demonstrator vehicles all of which carried G–– WAC registration plates. They are of some interest, particularly if in good condition, but they're not worth a premium. One that we'd all like to find is the very first Discovery, but unfortunately that's rather unlikely; at present, G794 BKW resides at the Heritage Motor Centre at Gaydon, where it's been since 1989, when it was taken straight there from the factory floor.

Build quality

Sad to say, but Discovery build quality was never the best in the world, though it improved markedly with the Series 2 models and beyond. Exterior panel fit on the early models was always a bit hit and miss, as was much of the interior trim, which tended to squeak and rattle even when new. This is another reason to take an expert with you – someone who will understand what is typical of the car in question and what may pose more of a problem.

← The decision about which Discovery model to buy will depend largely on your budget. Early examples of the Discovery 3 will have lost a huge proportion of their original value due to depreciation, but will still be out of reach for many people. A 2003 model, as shown here, makes perfect sense for those wanting a vehicle that's not too old and yet not too expensive, and examples may still be found at Land Rover dealerships.

> **DID YOU KNOW?**
> Like most large and, initially, expensive vehicles, the Discovery tends to lose lots of its value in the first few years. If you can live with 'pre-owned' you can save a heap of cash and still get a nearly-new car.

Which model?

It's a natural progression that the Series 2 (and latterly the Series 3) cars are the biggest, most accomplished, most technologically advanced, most comfortable, most powerful, most frugal – you get the picture. Trouble is, they're also the most expensive and for most buyers they're rather beyond the cash limit.

The 300 series 'facelift' models of the Series 1 and Series 2 models are currently the best balance of price versus sophistication and many are still young enough not to need any major mechanical work or to have suffered too badly from the dreaded tin-worm. If diesel is your choice, try a post-1996 model with the automatic ZF gearbox, as these had a few more bhp to help replace those few ponies soaked-up by the self-shifter.

The oldest of the 200 models are 20 years old, which means they're likely to have had one careful owner – and several not-so-careful ones! The rigid servicing regime carried out early in its life will probably have gone by the board and time will be taking its toll in every area. Having said that, a good 200 model is still a good buy, and although not as smooth and polished as the later models it will still perform very well on and off-road – and, of course, without the ballast of swingeing road tax penalties applied to newer models.

Buying

SOME GENERAL TIPS:

- See the car at the buyer's house – anyone trying to sell a stolen car or a 'ringer' (a car with a false identity) will usually prefer to meet you somewhere else, or come to your house.
- Many crafty thieves park outside someone else's house and just 'happen to be outside with the car' (washing it, maybe) when you arrive, so you assume that the house is theirs. Always try to get inside the house if you can – asking to go to the loo is fair. If the seller hasn't got the keys ('my daughter has them and has just gone to the supermarket' etc), be extremely wary.
- A keen owner will know where all the controls are – an 'owner' fumbling around for basics is a warning sign.
- The more paperwork, the better, especially MoT certificates, which are essential in plotting a car's true mileage.

THE BUYER'S TOOL KIT

- A torch, which lights up awkward nooks and crannies and makes you look like a serious buyer.
- A mat or carpet to kneel on when looking underneath.
- A magnet, to check that what should be steel isn't rust or filler.

← Look for signs of corrosion everywhere. This is where the steel corner of the car meets the steel upright.

↑ It's starting to bubble up around this rear lamp cluster – all the usual places, I'm afraid.

→ This section just above the rear bumper is a natural water-trap that encourages rust.

↑ **The steel rear floor can easily corrode. Moisture is held onto it by the carpet and thick layer of soundproofing, creating ideal conditions for rust.**

- A notepad, with a list of salient questions and points.
- Your own detailed list of what the standard specification ought to be.
- An assistant, preferably knowledgeable.
- A good idea of typical prices in your area – they vary across the country.

WHEN TO BUY

Plan your ownership carefully; study what there is and decide what you want. Ideally, buy your car in the summer months, for five main reasons:

1. There's lots more light, which means you can view with some confidence in the evenings.
2. It is (or should be) warmer, so you'll be more likely to take your time and thus spot potential problem areas.
3. It is (or should be …) drier, so you'll be more inclined to grovel around on the ground looking for underbody damage, oil leaks, rust and rot, worn bushes, etc.
4. Psychologically, people buy cabrios and sports cars in the summer and anything with four-wheel drive in the winter. It follows that the prices of four-wheel drive vehicles will be more during the winter months and less in the summer – which is the time to buy your Discovery.
5. If the worst happens and you do buy a car that requires work, it's less hardship sorting it out when you're not knee-deep in snow and fighting a –7° wind chill factor.

WHAT TO BUY

By definition, Series 1 cars are the oldest and so the cheapest and, as one would expect, not so refined as the later cars. In terms of engine, you've a choice of 3.5-litre or 3.9-litre V8 petrol or 2.5-litre diesel engines. It's difficult to resist the power, torque, and lovely sound of a V8, but they are thirsty units, even with fuel injection (which applies to all but the very first models – avoid carburettors if you can). Realistically, you can't expect more than 15mpg as an annual average, and when driven hard or off-roaded this can easily plummet below double figures. With UK petrol taxed at its current exorbitant rate, make sure you do some sums before you go for this option. However, you could have it converted to run on LPG (liquefied petroleum gas), when it would become easily as economical as a diesel-engined car whilst retaining all the good points of the 8-cylinder lump. Remember to build the conversion cost into your budget, which shouldn't be too difficult because V8-engined cars are usually much cheaper than their diesel equivalents. Swapping a V8 to a diesel engine is quite common, but far from cheap, and again demands some long nights with a spreadsheet before you consider it; it's often cheaper and always simpler to buy a diesel-powered Discovery in the first place.

The diesel option was always the more popular, with well over 80 per cent of all Discovery sales being derv-drinkers. Add to that the fact that the most popular Discovery body style was the five-door and you'll realise that when looking for a five-door diesel you're going to be spoilt for choice. This popularity generally makes them more available. The 200 Tdi engine was fitted to all pre-facelift cars and though its successor was identical in capacity and output, it was a very different unit.

The Mpi is relatively rare and certainly an acquired taste. It lacks low-down torque from its high-revving 16v Rover engine (despite a mid-term uprate) and isn't really suited to pulling around two tonnes of Land Rover. They're quite cheap to buy and not too expensive to run or insure, but make sure you drive one for some distance before parting with your cash – most drivers find the lack of low-down grunt too much to cope with after a few miles.

If you've a need to carry passengers on a regular basis, the five-door models make life so much easier. Inward-facing sixth and seventh rear seats were fitted to most models, so the odds are you'll get them whether you want them or not; there's enough around so there's no need to pay extra for them. Remember, though, that when they're occupied there's precious little space for luggage. And when folded, you lose the side bins as a place to store knick-knacks.

All models were produced with five-speed manual gearboxes, but automatic options were phased-in through its production run, from 1992 onwards on the V8i models and from 1993 onwards on diesel-powered cars. (An auto option was never available on the low-torque Mpi Discoverys.) The V8 engine is ideally suited to the automatic option – the sweet-performing ZF unit – but the rather clunky manual 'box has always seemed a bit at odds with the silky smooth eight-cylinder unit. Conversely, diesel engines tend to work better with the manual gearbox, not least because the lack of power compared to the petrol engine makes the car even more sluggish in general performance terms.

The 300 series cars (the facelift models from 1994) were more refined inside, with airbag and ABS options, a new and more modern dashboard,

and generally higher equipment levels. The 300 Tdi engine was also more suited to a vehicle with upmarket aspirations, if not quite as smooth overall as some of its opposition. Gearbox gremlins continued to plague the early 300s, though by now the faults should all have been rectified. As the launch of the Series 2 car drew closer, Land Rover soaked up the remaining supply of Series 1 300s by issuing a plethora of special editions which aren't worth that much extra per se, though the extras included as standard could make them more desirable than a less well-equipped model of similar vintage.

Oh, and don't forget that Discoverys – that's all models – are tall vehicles; check before you buy that it will actually fit in your garage!

PRE-BUYING CHECKS

It's advisable to check the provenance of any car you intend to buy with one of the agencies listed below – before you hand any money over. Some Land Rover magazines run their own schemes. It really doesn't matter which you choose, as long as you check the provenance with somebody. Some buyers may try to pressure a sale, but remember, there's plenty of good

↓ The bottom of this door is showing archetypal signs of electrolytic corrosion as the steel of the inner door reacts unfavourably with the aluminium of the outer door skin.

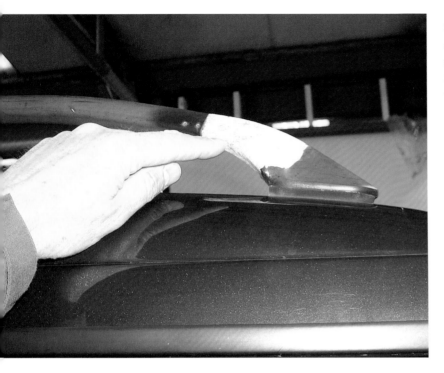

numbers, the vehicle colour, in which country it was originally registered, or if it has been written off at some point. The (current) cost of around £35 is nothing compared to the possible loss of many thousands of pounds.

HPI Equifax
Tel: 01722 413434
Website: www.hpicheck.com

AA Used Car Data Check
Tel: 0870 600 0838
Website: www.theaa.com

RAC
Tel: 0870 533 3660
Website: www.rac.co.uk

There are various 'levels' of writing off, the lowest (D) being a case where a vehicle is written off because it is not financially viable to repair it using manufacturers' original parts. The highest is 'A', and such vehicles should not be able to get back into circulation. However, modern car theft is a highly profitable business and thieves often find ways to bypass the laws of the land. There are two important points to consider, the first being that whilst, say, a schedule D car may only have required superficial work to bring it back to full roadworthiness, it still

↑ **This roof rail illustrates how aluminium corrodes. It doesn't actually rust, but when the surface is exposed to the elements (as here when the paint flaked off) the surface begins to pit and turn to a white powder. Where steel and aluminium meet (on the doors, for example), electrolytic reaction causes both metals to corrode.**

Discoverys around and if you lose this one, there'll be another along soon.

According to the AA's records, every 12 seconds they come across a vehicle that needs further investigation. A call to one of the organisations listed here will reveal such things as its presence on the stolen vehicle register, whether there is finance owing, a confirmation of the chassis and engine

→ **The large rear door proved to be too heavy for its hinges on early models, and they were subsequently beefed up. The release catch and central locking on the rear door often gave real hassles. Because of access difficulties, effecting what should be a simple repair isn't quite as easy as it should be.**

shows up on the computer records and so its value must be lowered accordingly. Equally, the only way to be absolutely sure that any such vehicle is sound is to have a full and complete check, such as those offered by the motoring organisations. This is not a cheap operation and the overall advice has to be to leave well alone – after all, the Discovery is hardly a rare car!

Try to get all the details you can from the vendor on the phone beforehand. It shows an honest seller that you're genuinely interested and a crook that he should beware. Make it clear you'll want to drive the vehicle even if only for a short distance (make sure you have insurance cover). In addition, ask that the engine should be cold when you get there, so you can see whether it starts well, and state that you will need to see the V5 (log book). If the V5 is not available do not buy the car. There may be a genuine reason for it being missing, but without it you can't double check the details you need to. Mention that you will be checking with one of the vehicle-check companies – a shifty seller will probably baulk at this point.

STAND AND STARE

Lots of people just leap in and drive off when buying a car, but there's lots to do before you even turn the engine over. Start with a visual check; from across the street it should look good, sitting four-square with no obvious leaning and with no nasty oil or coolant puddles beneath it. As you walk round the car, look hard at the paintwork for evidence of respraying (such as 'orange peel' effect, dull patches, slight colour mismatches, etc). Kneeling and looking right along the flanks of the car will get you some odd glances, but it will also reveal even the slightest imperfections. Don't be too harsh here, because the aluminium panels are easily damaged and Discoverys suffer more than most from the attentions of carelessly opened doors from adjacent vehicles. If it looks down-at-heel and neglected, then it probably is; many drivers buy them, believing they can run them on a Ford Fiesta budget – and find they can't.

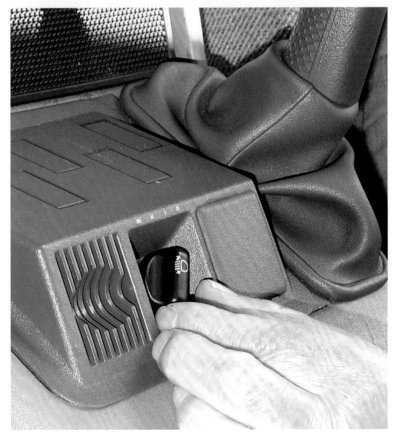

↑ Electrical goodies are great, as long as they work, so check that all such gear works as it should. This Discovery was very much a base model with no electric windows (though the blanks can be seen), but it had the optional headlamp levelling feature, which compensates for high headlamp angles when towing heavy loads. The system uses a solenoid at the back of each headlamp, so, like everything else, it's important to check that they work.

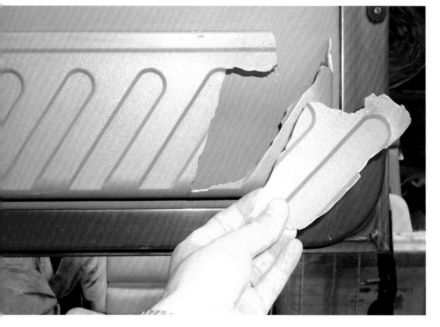

of the various component parts, not only between Discoverys, but between Defenders and Range Rovers, makes life easy for the thief.

BODYWORK

Almost all the Discovery outer bodywork is aluminium (Birmabright). It can't rust, but moisture does cause it to corrode over time, bubbling the paintwork and leaving a white powdery finish. It's also a soft material and prone to marking easily. A Discovery without the odd car parking 'ding' is probably one that hasn't left the showroom. But if there's lots of damage, however, it might mean the car has been badly driven or heavily off-roaded. If the latter, it will have taken its toll in other areas too. Remember that beneath the aluminium is steel and where the two metals meet, you get electrolytic reaction which leads to corrosion and is particularly evident on the door skins/frames.

The doors should all open and shut with a solid clunk and not drop slightly as they're opened. On five-door models it's not uncommon to find the rear doors seizing in their hinges, particularly where the car has been owned by someone without a family. Apply the same test to the rear door remembering that the huge spare wheel/tyre attached to it, gives those hinges a hard time. Early models in particular were prone to rear door-drop and most rear door locks give trouble at some stage – in essence, it's a simple task to sort, but getting at the collection of rods and connections within the door is tricky to say the least. It's common for the central locking to work on the passenger doors but not at the rear – physically checking is the simplest way to make sure everything is OK.

INSIDE

The trim was never of the best quality and the plastics in particular were very flimsy and easy to damage. As such, a car where the interior trim is in good condition *and* undamaged is quite rare, not least since most owners don't bother to replace damaged trim on the grounds that the new part will probably last no longer than the original. The seat material is generally quite hard-wearing, but will probably be fraying round the edges on high-mileage examples. Similarly, plastic graining on the steering wheel and gear knob can smooth over when lots of miles have been covered.

In terms of 'accessories', look for the most you can get for your money, with official Land Rover kit being preferred. Most cars came with electric windows,

↑ ↑ Discovery plastics have never been the best in the world, though they did improve over time. This plastic section which secures the rear carpet is exactly where you place any load intended for the luggage bay. Why it wasn't metal we can only guess.

↑ The map-style pocket fitted to some rear doors is an excellent idea and great for storing useful bits and pieces, especially when the twin rear seat option has been specified. But again, the plastic is prone to breaking.

PAPERWORK

If you're happy it looks right, then it's on to the paperwork – note this is still before you drive the car. If the V5 (log book) isn't present, come back when it is. It's a common con-trick for it to be lost, machine-washed, eaten by the dog, etc. Check the number of owners, that the description matches the vehicle (colour, number of doors, etc), the exact age, and that the chassis and engine numbers tally. Remember that the VIN number can tell you exactly what the vehicle should be, and by cross-referencing with the information given in the Appendix you'll be able to do a quick double-check. Does the VIN plate show signs of tampering? Be suspicious, because Discoverys are notoriously easy to ring – ie to give a false identity. The interchangeability

central locking, seven seats, and twin sunroofs, the more so with younger cars, so they shouldn't make much difference to the price. Air conditioning does add a premium to the car but take great care to make sure that it works properly – a thorough overhaul can cost well over £1,000. And remember that when it's switched on, it will increase fuel consumption. Without doubt, leather trim is a bonus, but don't pay too much for it as you can easily uprate from a specialist such as Nationwide Trim or by getting second-hand original equipment trim from a 4 x 4 breaker.

If you're looking at a 300 series from 1994/5/6 then check the top of the dashboard carefully. Land Rover has admitted that some tops were fitted using a faulty glue and agree to replace the dash if necessary. One would expect all affected cars to have been sorted by now, but it's worth looking out for.

In-car electrics – central locking, electric windows, etc – are always nice to have, but make sure they all work exactly as they should, because replacements are expensive. This applies particularly to any security system fitted. Over time, Land Rover fitted their own systems, both immobilisers and combined immobiliser/alarms. Be sure that everything works and if there is a remote control, test it thoroughly – and make sure you take the spare as well. If an aftermarket system has been installed, make sure it has been done professionally – DIY alarm fitments are not to be recommended. If the security is Thatcham recommended, you'll need an installation certificate in order to convince your insurers, who may then give away a little discount. If you're looking at a car with air conditioning, pay great attention – make sure it works in every single mode because, as already mentioned, repair and servicing is extremely expensive, and impossible to complete on a DIY basis. Many owners turn the system off for long periods of time in order to save a little on fuel, but this is short-sighted and does the set-up no good at all.

UNDERBONNET

The engine bay should look as if someone cares for the engine – if there's a layer of oily grime 10mm thick, it's time to go home. Not only has there been a careless owner, but that grime can cover a multitude of sins, from massive oil leaks to cracked chassis and damaged coolant pipes, etc. Check the oil, coolant,

↑ **All engines should be basically oil-free on the outside, but be topped up with clean stuff when you check the dipstick. Look at all fluids for levels, and make sure the various air hoses are intact on the turbo diesel models.**

brake fluid and, where applicable, automatic gearbox levels. (The auto box dipstick is in the engine bay. Note that there are different markers on it depending on the engine temperature; check the handbook for specific details. Of course, a caring owner should know what these are.) The levels should be spot-on and the fluids should look fresh (always tricky to gauge on a diesel engine, as the oil seems to go jet black almost immediately). Remove the engine oil filler cap and look inside. You don't want to see a white, foamy mayonnaise which could indicate a blown head gasket – an expensive repair operation on petrol or diesel. Discovery steering boxes are a known weak point, so pay special attention here. The reservoir should be at the right level with no obvious leaks – it's an MoT failure point and replacement is expensive, wherever you buy.

Look around the inner wings, which are known to rot through over time, and look hard around the lower parts of the engine bay for signs of a front-end crash (creased metal, paint over-spray, etc).

TDI ENGINES

Before you lift the bonnet you need to know when the cam belt was last changed. Discoverys are prone to cam belt failure and the resulting damage as pistons and valves get together is extremely expensive. If there's no evidence it's been done recently, build the cost of a change into the price you pay. Like any diesel, it will rattle more when cold, but it shouldn't vibrate overmuch, though a 300 engine should be less vibratory and slightly quieter than the earlier unit. Check the condition of all pipes and hoses, as they can often work loose over time.

The Tdi needs oil changing at least every 6,000 miles (9,600km), something not all owners realise, so again make sure you add this in to your estimate of running costs. You can use the idle test as a check on its general condition; let the warmed engine idle for a few minutes, then blip the throttle

sharply, looking in the mirror (or with an associate standing behind the car). If you see great clouds of black smoke, it indicates trouble somewhere – possibly a tune-up will solve the problem but, equally, it could be more serious internal engine wear.

V8 ENGINES

As Chris Crane at RPi confirms, the most important servicing aspect of the Rover V8 engine is regular oil-changing. An engine which has had regular changes/filters will rumble happily on towards 200,000 miles. However, neglect this simple task and you're in trouble; sludgy oil deposits start to form which start by messing up the cam and continue from there. Dip your fingers into the oil filler aperture (on a cold engine!) and if they come out covered in black sludge, walk smartly away.

BUYING CHECKLIST

This list should be used as a basic guide in conjunction with the more detailed sections appearing elsewhere in this chapter.

Location, location, location
Try and view at the owner's home. Meeting in car parks, etc, is suspicious – the car may be stolen. Check its regular parking place for signs of oil/coolant leaks.

Is the log book (V5) present? Don't accept that it was swallowed by the dog or eaten by the washing machine.
Stop now! Do not buy a Discovery of any hue without seeing the V5 (see next comment).

Check the name/address, number of owners, engine, chassis, and VIN numbers, etc, on the V5.
Any discrepancies should be ironed out before continuing. Use the Appendix to ensure it's the correct model and hasn't been doctored in some way.

Is there at least some service history, invoices, etc? Ensure that the mileages tally.
Older cars probably won't be dealer-serviced, but enthusiasts tend to keep every single invoice for parts replaced and service items bought; the less there is, the more you should worry.

17RA	04150	68R	4CYL DIESEL MAN	000052
34R	01007	68R	V8 PETROL MAN	000053
45R	01007	68R	4CYL PETROL MAN	000054
68R	000051	68R	4CYL DIESEL AUTO	000055
	V8 PETROL AUTO			

Are there MoT certificates? Ensure that the mileages tally.

Again, enthusiasts hoard these, and if present they give some idea of the true mileage.

VIEWING

Is it raining or has it rained recently? Has the car just been washed?

Bear this in mind. Water makes any car's paintwork look better than it is.

Are you viewing in fading light?

You really can't inspect a car properly in the dark or half-light.

Look hard all around the car.

Check along its flanks for accident damage. Check inside the boot and engine bay for minor bumps. Check for signs of paint over-spraying, etc.

Look in the engine bay. Check oil and coolant levels.

Dirty oil or brown coolant are worrying signs, as are oil leaks and a generally scruffy bay.

Look under the car.

Check for oil leaks from the engine, transmission, or dampers. Look under wheel arches and along the sills for damage or rust. Check exhaust condition.

Wheels and tyres

Check wheels for serious damage – expect minor scuffs. Check tyres for legal tread, uneven patterns, sidewall damage, etc.

Look at brake discs and pads through wheels.

Damaged and/or scored discs and badly worn pads mean no test-drive until replaced. You should know the cost of replacements.

Interior trim

Check condition is commensurate with mileage. Look for signs of abuse. Remember, Discovery trim was never the finest even when new.

Interior functions

Make sure everything electrical works, especially expensive kit such as air conditioning.

↑ Numbers on the V5 logbook and the VIN plate should match perfectly. Check for obvious signs of tampering. You'll also get important vehicle information here relating to weights, exact paint colour etc.

DRIVING

Start the car and let it idle.

The car should start easily and idle cleanly straight away – if not, there could be fuel-injection or electronic problems.

If possible, drive the car on a selection of road surfaces.

Check all gears engage and stay there. Listen for untoward noises from engine/suspension.

Braking

Brakes should stop the car quickly and in a straight line. Check ABS warning light operation (where fitted) – incorrect function is an MoT failure point.

After the test drive

Let the engine idle for a few minutes, then blip the throttle – a puff of blue smoke indicates engine wear and lots of expense.

Check the provenance – use HPI, AA, RAC, or any company offering similar facilities. A cost of (currently) around £35 could save you many thousands.

An essential phone call which reveals if the car has been stolen, written-off, still has finance against it, etc, even against a changed 'personal' number plate.

The deal

Like an auction, set your budget beforehand and stick to it. Know replacement prices and use them as a lever to get to your price. Offset against any spares included in the deal.

The choice

The car you buy has to be the right one for you at the right price. Never forget that there are thousands of Discoverys for sale now. If you're not totally sure, walk away and find another.

Conversions

Many Discoverys have had their original V8 petrol engines removed and a diesel engine slotted in its place. These cars need approaching with caution. The best conversion is that which uses Land Rover's own engine and kit of parts (engine mountings etc). It's more popular (because it's cheaper) to use a Japanese engine of some description, some of which work better than others.

Liquefied petroleum gas conversions are becoming increasingly popular. The quality of installation varies alarmingly as there are few hard and fast rules and hardly any legislation. An expert is a must when looking at an LPG converted petrol car. Think about where the LPG tank is sited and whether or not it will affect how you want to use it; if it is in the luggage area, it could mean that the rear seat(s) cannot be used. If under the front floors, it could limit the car's use off-road. The size of the tank is important, especially if you live in an area where LPG is in limited supply.

With any conversion, check the attitude of your insurers before you buy. All are likely to want, at the very least, an engineer's report as to the quality of installation, safety aspects, and whether or not the brakes and suspension should be uprated as a result of the change. A typical example is where the relatively lightweight all-alloy V8 is swapped for a cast-iron diesel, which requires that the front suspension should be beefed up accordingly.

↓ **Don't try this at home! Rather an extreme illustration of just what a Discovery's suspension can cope with.** (Nick Dimbleby)

→ **This is the front differential and is typical of most you'll see, with a light covering of oil resulting in the occasional driveway drip. Expect little better, but if you can see a steady drip, drip, drip after a test run, bargain for repair work.**

Transmission

GEARBOXES

If you're not clued-up on how Land Rover products should work, it's advisable to take along someone who is. The gearboxes were never quiet and to anyone used to modern Euro-hatchbacks and their slick-shifting cogs, they can feel clunky and unrefined. Don't take gearbox problems lightly, as almost everything means removing the 'box, which is a lengthy procedure. It isn't the sort of thing you can do on your driveway, or even in a well-equipped garage. Of course, a worn/damaged/recalcitrant 'box can be an excellent bargaining point and if used correctly can be your way to getting a good car cheaper, after which gearbox specialists such as LEGS can soon sort out a replacement.

MANUAL

With the engine running, the car in neutral, and your foot off the clutch, listen for a gearbox rattle which could be a layshaft problem. There should be no baulking when selecting a gear, and once selected gears should stay there – check especially the lower two, as they're the ones that get the most hammered and are most likely to jump out. Once engaged, there's usually a measure of noise, but it shouldn't be excessive. As with most vehicles, first and second gears get used most and are more likely to be worn, especially the synchromesh. Look for an easy change from fifth to fourth gear – baulking here indicates some rebuild work required.

To check for mainshaft or transfer 'box problems, pull up steadily, stop the car, and engage reverse gear. As you let the clutch pedal up, listen for a harsh, metallic clack from the back of the gearbox – roughly underneath the driver's left elbow. If you hear it, there could be trouble ahead. Transfer box input gear problems were rife on early 300 cars. Though intended to address the problems found in the LT77/S gearbox, the R380 had its own fair share, especially in early 300 series cars. There were many hassles reported with the synchromesh and, of course, the most famous (or infamous!) one of all was the lack of mainshaft lubrication. Land Rover itself produced

a modification to solve the input gear and mainshaft problems and some aftermarket companies have sorted similar solutions. You should be able to hear any serious problems, and in truth, the problems usually occurred so early in the car's life that they should have been sorted by now. But play it safe – if you're not sure, get an expert's opinion.

AUTOMATIC

Auto 'boxes should make progress smoother and less agricultural with barely noticeable changes.

↑ **It's a similar story under the main and transfer gearboxes. An oil haze can be found on most Land Rover gearboxes; it's when the fluid leaks like a tap that you have to worry. How well the various 'boxes actually work is the important factor.**

↑ All models were fitted with power steering, the pump of which was prone to leaks. The odd weep is par for the course but anything more means expensive replacement and, again, an MoT failure.

↑ Suspension is conventional all-round, being simple dampers and springs. At the rear, however, the springs and dampers are separate units, making replacement easier.

→ A brief glance under the front shows that the newly-fitted Scorpion springs and dampers need no attention. But there's the steering arm, Panhard rod, and front-to-rear radius arms all congregating in much the same area. Rubber bushes are used aplenty, and when worn create a feel of very sloppy handling. The ball-end joints are standard issue and wear as you'd expect. Later models may well have an anti-roll bar to complicate things further.

Make sure the 'box changes into top, then hit the accelerator hard to ensure that the kick-down facility works properly. Select D, 1, 2, and 3 manually and make sure that the gears are held correctly. The Tdi engines always had to work hard with all that weight to carry and they had to work even harder with an auto transmission. This means that auto acceleration will seem rather dull in comparison with the manual gearbox. The German-made ZF boxes fitted to Discoverys have an excellent reputation for performance and reliability. As such, any problems are usually glaringly obvious.

LOW BOX

All Discoverys have a second set of gear ratios, much lower than normal (a ratio of 2:1). They're intended for serious off-roading or working in mud or snow. They're also very useful for reversing with a large trailer. Make sure you check that the low-ratio lever (the little stubby one) engages correctly and that you can get the full five (plus reverse) gears. If the centre differential lock is manual, engage that and ensure that the warning light illuminates – but only drive a few yards on tarmac, otherwise you'll cause axle wind-up, which places extra strain on the drive components and chews the tyres up badly. You will usually have to drive a couple of yards after de-selecting the differential lock before you see the light extinguish – this is normal.

Suspension and steering

Discoverys weigh over two tonnes, which means there's a lot of car to support and that dampers and springs need to be up to the job. Though every Discovery will roll more than a normal saloon (not least because of the extra height) it should still feel controlled and not uneven in any way. The car should sit level all the way around, and if it doesn't, replacements are due. Down on your knees, check for signs of leaking from the dampers, and if you see plenty of rust on them they're clearly getting old.

The Discovery suspension is fairly conventional. Replacements are inexpensive and there's lots of choice from standard to seriously hard, but nevertheless, it's a bargaining point. While you're under the front end, look at the steering balls on each side, which should be oily on the parts where the steering can't reach and shiny silver where it can. Signs of rusting means they've been allowed to run dry and will need replacing – not cheap and quite involved to do.

More serious is the condition of the many rubber bushes. Under the Discovery is an absolute plethora of heavy-duty arms and rods designed to keep the car pointing in the right direction and these are supported by a series of rubber bushes. By the time the car is, say, five years old, these will be well-worn and ready for changing. If they haven't been, swapping the lot can be a costly exercise, especially as DIY-changing isn't really an option for many of the bushes – you'll need a very capable bearing press for a start. If you're changing the bushes, it's well worth considering upgrading to Polybushes; these polyurethane replacements are far tougher, will last longer, and will control the roll of the car far better than the original rubber items.

← Even without the aid of a ramp, you can get on your knees and check the condition of the steering swivel balls. They should be shiny, as here, with no signs of rust-pitting in the silver balls themselves. If there is, it indicates that the swivel balls have been allowed to run dry of oil. Once rust has taken hold the balls must be replaced, because the uneven surface will soon wreck the seals ...

← ... and the result will be something like this. Replacement is a messy, fiddly job and not cheap, and should always be done in pairs.

Brakes

Stopping all that weight requires plenty of braking power. All models were equipped with twin circuit, servo-assisted brakes, which work well regardless of model. Later models may be equipped with ABS anti-lock braking, which was an option for some years. The brakes should stop the car quickly, without drama and without pulling

→ Try to get a look at the condition and, better still, the thickness of the discs and pads, which should have plenty of meat on them. Rear callipers often seize because of their relative lack of use. When driving, it's hard to tell, so physically looking to see that the pads are wiping the rust off the disc is the simplest way to check.

→ Some 300 series Discoverys were fitted with a Wabco anti-lock brake (ABS) system. This is obviously a plus point. Check that the ABS light in the console comes on with the ignition and then goes off after a few seconds. If it stays on while you're driving, it means trouble and an MoT failure.

to either side. The rear brakes in particular tend to get little use as most braking effort goes to the front. The result can be seized callipers, the best answer for which is replacement. Try to get a look at the discs and check the general condition. If there's a large lip around the edge, then the disc is very worn and probably due for replacement – of course, always replace discs in axle sets with new pads. Look around the callipers and at the brake pipes/unions in general for signs of fluid leakage. Check the operation of

the servo by sitting in the car with the engine off and pressing hard on the brake pedal. Start the engine and as the servo kicks in, the pedal should go down noticeably. If it stays hard, then the servo is not functioning correctly.

Wheels and tyres

Alloys look better but are easier to damage and more expensive to replace. Official Land Rover wheels are favourite, as you can be sure they're up to the job of carting around such a heavy vehicle – especially important when off-roading. Check around all the rims for signs of heavy kerbing, especially with alloys, which are more expensive to repair/replace. Check the tyre tread and around the sidewalls; damage here can't be repaired and good tyres are not cheap. The tyres should be the same size at each corner (don't laugh …) and, ideally, the same type. A mix'n'match indicates someone trying to run the car on a shoestring; and if they're saving cash on this vital area of safety, where else have corners been cut? Cheap tyres are a false economy and if those fitted are not recognised as being ideal for the car, allow for a set of (at least) four in your budget.

At the front, make sure that the tyres are wearing evenly. There's plenty of rods and joints under the front of the Discovery, and all have to be spot-on to make the car handle and steer correctly. In addition, it's common for the pre-load on the front steering balls to be incorrect, causing wheel-wobble (often thought to be the fault of a perfectly good steering damper) and, of course, uneven tyre wear.

Under the car

The most important item under the car is the ladder chassis, two great box sections of steel running from front to rear of the car. Everything is either bolted to or hung from this. Check the two main rails and then the outriggers which extend at various points. The body bolts to these, so it's important. A really weak area is the rear crossmember, which is unfortunate, as it's structural. Run a gloved

← Nice original equipment, Freestyle alloy wheels with equally impressive Pirelli tyres. Not all Discoverys are so well-endowed in the wheels and tyres department. Check tyre condition carefully.

↓ Wobbles and shakes from the front end being transmitted up the steering wheel are common. If you're looking, it could be that the steering damper has failed – this is quite a cheap and simple repair. However, it's also possible that the steering swivel pre-load needs adjusting, and this is a much more complex procedure.

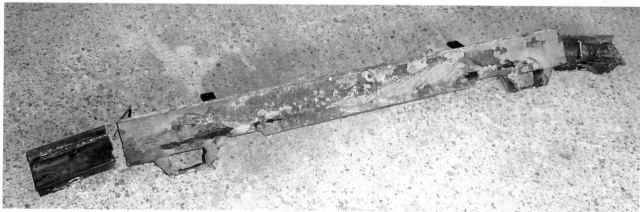

hand right up behind the rear bumper (it's a dirty job) and prod hard with your fingers. I've seen eight-year-old cars with serious rot right the way along here, so ignore this test at your peril. It can be replaced, but it's a very involved operation requiring an expert's skill, which means you pay an expert's money.

Look for rust/rot along the floors on each side, particularly the front arches and foot wells and rear arches. As a rule, floors can be patch welded without too much difficulty, and there

are proprietary repair panels for just about everything under the car that's likely to rust.

At the rear of the car, the fuel tanks are plastic and all but impossible to mend, but they don't corrode, so they're usually less hassle. Of course, they're still vulnerable to off-road damage, so check them for damage just the same.

There's lots of ground clearance so there's no reason for not having a good look at the condition of the exhaust system. Make sure it's hanging correctly from the chassis hooks (they

↑ The rear crossmember sits in front of the rear bumper, behind the fuel tank, and is hard to see without some effort on your part. It is vital to the structure of the car and prone to disintegrating. This is one that had to be cut away completely – make sure you don't buy a car with one like this!

↑ In common with the Defenders and the Range Rover, the Discovery tends to rust holes in its front passenger foot wells. These are usually fairly simple to sort out, using proprietary panels from any specialist and the skills of a good welder.

↑ It's a good idea to check along both sills and the rear wheel arches. Look also at the condition of all fuel lines and brake pipes, which are not only MoT failures but extremely important safety points.

↑ A typical front catalyst – ie, very rusty. These things are costly to replace and difficult to tell if they're working. A test at a MoT station (which will have the complex electronic kit required) is the only way to be sure.

↑ The Discovery exhaust system isn't particularly complicated but it's large and there's plenty of it, which means possible imminent replacement is something to build into the purchase price.

can rot quite easily) and that there are no signs of heavy rust or blowing from existing holes or patched repairs. Remember that from 1993, petrol-engined Discoverys had to be fitted by law with catalyst exhaust systems, which are extremely expensive to replace, and a good one is essential in order to pass the MoT test. One that's really shot will actually rattle, but often they can fail quietly. If the car has a long MoT then you might want to risk it. However, if the current MoT expires soon, then it would be worth asking the buyer to have it tested – even if you stump up the test fee, which is considerably less than the cat cost.

Insurance

Shop around is the obvious advice. Check out the adverts in the specialist magazines (at the time of writing there were four dealing solely with Land Rover's products) and remember that you can cut your costs by opting for a limited mileage policy. If you're intending to off-road your car, check the policy small print as some will exclude it. Remember also that when driving on an official green lane, you are technically still on a public highway, so your insurance must be valid. Most Discoverys have seven seats, so don't tell your insurer that it has five, and if you're going to be doing the school-run, ensure your policy doesn't class it as being taxi driving and exclude cover.

Paying the price

The various buying guides will give you a good starting point, though prices will vary with the area you're in. Buying from a Land Rover dealer means you pay a premium but should get a comprehensive warranty to ease the financial pain. However, the franchises only handle younger/low-mileage cars, so a raft of 'specialist' dealers has sprung up to cope with those cars that fall through the net. There are some very good ones around, but equally, there's plenty of cowboys ready to lasso the unwary. Take your time, check around and look for personal recommendations if you can. Buying privately is a cheaper way still to buy a car, but of course, you've no warranty and, as long as the car wasn't falsely described, no comeback at all. This is where you need to know your onions, or alternatively, take someone who does.

This applies even more so to the very cheapest way to buy – at an auction. Buying at a general sale is OK, but limits your options. Probably the best choice is a specialist 4x4 auction, such as those at Brightwells in Leominster. By definition, it's the buying method with most risk, but the savings are enormous: it's easy to save £2–5,000 depending on the model you want, which means that you'll have a large cash margin to soak up any possible problems. Inspection time is limited and you're unlikely to be able to drive the cars, although some auctions will allow the engine to be started. You'll need to have your cash/ card ready to pay and have some insurance sorted so you can drive home – unless you trailer it. Warranty is typically just one hour and will cover only major problems – a five-speed gearbox which will only select three gears, for example. The two major rules are simple: know your stuff or take someone with you who does, and set a price limit before the auction starts and stick to it!

Discovery Series 2 and 3

The basic buying rules apply here – checking the V5, etc – but the S2 is a very different car to its predecessor. The rugged, repair-with-a-Swiss-Army-

Knife thinking behind the early cars was well and truly junked, with complex electronics ruling the roost. Many and various ECUs (electronic control units) took over a whole host of functions and when they fail, they're expensive. Repairing on a DIY basis is not possible for mere mortals, likewise performing checks to make sure they're working correctly. We have to advise that unless you really understand car electronic systems, buying an S2 with a cast-iron warranty is by far the best bet.

Buying an S3 Discovery demands more than ever that you follow all the usual rules with regard to checking and double-checking numbers, provenance and paperwork, because even at four–five years old, the price will still be considerable. Given the huge technological leaps made with this car, you are well-advised to invest £200–£300 in having a thorough examination made by an expert; this can be either via one of the major motoring organisations or by a specialist in the marque. Remember that even a 'simple' replacement ECU can cost over a thousand pounds, and there are few repairs that can be carried out at home.

↑ The rules regarding bull bars are covered in legislation 2005/66/EC. From this date, they are referred to as frontal protection systems (FPS) and the essence of the new type of 'bull bar' is that they must actively reduce pedestrian injuries on impact and, importantly, pass a series of tests to prove it. Each must carry an EU approval number permanently attached. FPS systems are effectively deeply padded versions of the original bars and designed in such a way as to direct force away from the pedestrian. From 25th May 2007, FPS had to comply to the new standard which effectively outlawed the old style metal bull bars. Cars registered after this date must have the new type of bar. However, cars made before that date can retain their metal bars.

CHAPTER 7
OWNING & RUNNING YOUR DISCOVERY

Unlike Solihull vehicles such as the Series Land Rovers or even the Defender range, all Discoverys are perfectly at home being used as 'everyday' cars, whether that's being used to carry bales of hay to sheep in a far-flung Welsh field or carry half a street full of kids to school. They're perfectly civilised inside, with comfortable and adjustable seats, room for five or seven people and/or lots of luggage, and that lofty driving position makes it fun and safe to drive. It's a big bonus, too, for children, who just love looking down on the world. Even with a basic specification, it's a pleasant environment, and a few extras, such as electric windows, air conditioning, or central locking, make it even more so. The relative frugality of the diesel engines at the pumps means you're not paying a premium for driving a superbly capable 4x4, and most drivers will be able to average 25+mpg. On long runs this could touch the hem of 30mpg although hard use and/or a spot of serious off-roading could result in figures nearer to 20mpg. The V8 is arguably the best engine to have at your disposal, although you'll also be disposing of large lumps of cash to the oil barons and the government (via the swingeing UK fuel tax) – expect to average around 15mpg for a typical driving mix. Whilst it's true that long journeys with a restrained right foot could add another 5mpg to this, it's also true that lots of city driving could see it drop below 12mpg. A day on an off-road course will probably see that figure drop down well into single figures.

At the time of writing, most Series 3 Discoverys would still be under warranty and be being serviced by Land Rover franchised dealers. Clearly, these cars are the most user-friendly of the range in terms of owning and driving, though with their preponderance of clever electronics on board, they will be very difficult to fix on a budget in years to come. Few of us could make any sense of a typical ECU in the way, say, that Mark Adams of Pharmhouse Marketing can, and this is a very

important point to bear in mind when considering a S2 model. As such, most of the advice provided in this chapter is applicable to S1 Discoverys, in both 200 and 300 guise.

Maintenance

According to 'a bloke down the pub', taking on a large 4x4 like the Discovery is akin to betting your life-savings on the turn of a card. OK, everyone's heard some horror stories, but of course, that applies to just about every car you can think of. However, as with any vehicle, if you buy the right car to start with you'll find that keeping your Discovery sweet can be very cost-effective. Most Series 1 Discoverys are quite old nowadays, but happily, they're also quite old-fashioned, and low-tech is good news for those who like to do their own maintenance. Even if you don't, they're relatively cheap for a specialist to work on.

Regular checks

To get the most out of your Discovery, and to keep it in tip-top condition, there are a few jobs you should do on a regular basis. We're not going to get into a 'how to do a full service' on your Discovery, as that would take up too much space, and there's an excellent Haynes Service and Repair Manual (number 3016) for the Discovery which tells you exactly what needs doing when, and how to do it.

The idea here is simply to tell you what needs regular attention, and what to check to ensure that

← If you use your Discovery in particularly hot or dusty conditions, you may need to reduce the mileage intervals between services. (Nick Dimbleby)

> **DID YOU KNOW?**
> If you get trouble with a propshaft or differential and really need to keep going, you can simply disconnect the propshaft and run on two-wheel drive. How versatile is that?

you are not let down by a problem that could easily have been avoided. So often one small thing can be overlooked, only for it to develop into a bigger, and often more expensive, problem later on. Most of the items that need to be checked regularly can be found under the bonnet – you shouldn't even have to get your hand dirty!

The first and most important regular check is the engine oil level, which ideally should be tested once a week. Always make sure your pride and joy is parked on level ground when you make the check, and wait at least five minutes after stopping the engine – to allow all the oil to run back into the sump – before you pull out the dipstick. Ideally, check it when the engine is stone cold. If you need to top up, make sure you use good-quality oil, and don't overfill. Remember, though, that the V8 engine was designed in a different age and with different tolerances to the modern diesels and that

all-singing synthetic is usually unnecessary; as a rule, a good quality 20w/50 or 10w/40 is fine.

The brake fluid level should be checked regularly too, especially if your Discovery gets a lot of off-road use. It's just possible that if you've been driving over rough terrain you could have damaged a brake hydraulic line – not a problem that you want to discover for the first time as you fail to stop at a busy junction! It's true that the car has dual circuit brakes, but the difference in braking ability when one of them is lost is massive. Brake fluid level will drop very slowly as the brake friction material wears, but you should hardly notice this, and any significant drop in fluid level indicates a leak somewhere in the system. In this case, don't drive the car until the problem has been found and fixed.

Whilst you're under the bonnet, it's wise to also check the coolant level. The level is checked in the expansion tank, and should always be checked with the engine cold. If you need to top up, remember that occasional use of plain water is OK, but if you add plain water regularly you'll dilute the strength of the coolant, which will reduce its anti-corrosion and anti-freeze properties. Remember that a 50 per cent mix of coolant and water is your aim;

↓ **It's the simplest underbonnet task you can think of, but checking and changing the oil regularly will pay handsomely. This is especially so with the V8, which will soon ruin its camshaft if it's left to spin in dirty oil. And …**

↑ ... whilst you can just about remove the cam with the engine in situ, it's not for the faint-hearted, and if it's badly worn due to a lack of clean oil there may be other problems elsewhere, not least ...

← ... worn main bearings. Compare the cost of oil and filter twice a year to that of a complete rebuild – no contest!

you can buy simple and cheap checkers from most DIY stores.

Keep the washer fluid level topped up. You can guarantee that if you don't the fluid will run out when you most need it, when driving on a salty winter road, or when following a tractor down a muddy lane. Add a reputable screen wash to help clean the screen and lower the freezing temperature.

Right, nearly there; just two more levels to check, namely power steering fluid and clutch fluid or automatic transmission fluid, depending on whether you have a manual or auto model. The power steering fluid is checked using a dipstick attached to the reservoir filler cap. The fluid level should be checked with the engine stopped, and the front wheels set in the straight-ahead position. The only reason for the fluid level being low is a leak. As mentioned, this is a common problem, although generally a weep will go for years before becoming serious – as long as the level is topped up regularly. To drive a Discovery without power steering you'll need the physique of a bodybuilder, so it's worth keeping an eye out for leaks. That physique will also come in handy when it comes to lifting the large wads of cash you'll need for replacement parts – a few extra drops of fluid are a lot cheaper.

If you have a model with automatic transmission, the fluid level should be checked regularly as recommended in the vehicle handbook or manual. Nine times out of ten automatic transmission problems are due to low fluid level. Finally, if your Discovery has a manual gearbox the clutch fluid level should be checked once in a while. Again, there should be no serious drop in fluid level during normal operation of the clutch, and a significant drop indicates a leak in the clutch hydraulic system.

That's all the underbonnet checks finished, but there are still a couple more checks that it's worth carrying out at least once a week. Check your tyre pressures: it's very easy to pick up a slow puncture

DID YOU KNOW?

There's a huge demand for stolen off-roaders in many Asian countries, where swingeing taxes make them largely unaffordable. Bribes to dodgy officials make illegal 'import' easy and profits huge – one more reason to pay close attention to your security precautions.

if you've been driving off-road. Always check the tyre pressures cold, and if possible always use the same gauge to check them – different gauges can often give surprisingly different readings. Try and get your own accurate gauge because forecourt gauges take a lot of mistreatment and are notoriously unreliable. Remember to include the spare, topping it up to 5–10psi more than is required, to allow for any change in pressure before it's needed; you can always let a few extra psi out.

The final check involves the wiper blades. All that's needed here is a quick examination to ensure that the blades are not split or damaged. It's worth renewing the blades once a year, even if they seem in good condition, as over time they tend to pick up grease from the road which will smear the glass, usually most noticeable when a car's coming towards you at night with its headlights glaring.

And that's it. It should only take ten minutes or so to carry out these checks, but it's time well spent which will help you to pick up on any problems before they develop into anything serious, and you'll have the peace of mind that you shouldn't have any nasty surprises on your next epic journey that could easily have been avoided.

V8 engines

The eight-cylinder Rover engine has been around for donkey's years, so there's a wealth of knowledge available and lots of outlets for spares. There's a key to keeping this lovely engine running sweetly and it's this: change the oil regularly! The engine is tolerant of just about all forms of use and abuse, but it will not stand being run with dirty old oil. A 10,000-mile (16,000km) change is maximum and OK if you do lots of miles in a year (where the engine/oil spends most of its time at the optimum temperature). However, if you're a low-mileage user (and many V8s tend to fall into this group because of the low mpg figures), then make that a 5,000-mile (8,000km) oil-change, and if you do a really low mileage, change it at least once a year. Without these changes the camshaft will wear its lobes to nothing in double-quick time, leading to predictable engine problems – and expense. All the metal shaved off the cam will find its way elsewhere, with damaged main bearings following

as night follows day. According to engine expert Holly at RPi Engineering, because the engine has its roots well beyond its first Rover usage in the 1960s there's no need to go over the top with fully synthetics – a good quality 20w-50 will do nicely.

Being all-aluminium, the engine doesn't take kindly to being overheated, so always make sure the coolant level is topped up. Just as importantly, in order to prevent corrosion in the waterways, blockages, and overheating, the coolant should be a 50/50 mixture of water and coolant (not anti-freeze anymore; modern coolant serves to lower the temperature at which it freezes and raise the temperature at which it boils) all year round. If the engine does overheat, you can expect warped cylinder heads, blowing head gaskets, and possibly a distorted engine block. On older engines, it's worth fitting aftermarket Kenlowe electronic fans to replace or even supplement the unwieldy viscous unit. The latter can lock solid, leading to gradual overheating problems.

If you have a Discovery with a catalytic exhaust system, then take heed! Cats are notoriously expensive to replace and, unlike conventional exhaust boxes, don't have to be rotted through to be useless. They're relatively fragile and if you knock one hard enough, it could be wrecked internally. It shouldn't affect the running of the car, because the engine management should compensate, but when it comes to MoT time, the emissions will be way too high and a 'fail' is inevitable. Purchasing another will not be a happy occasion – at the time of writing, the official price was well over £1,000 – though you can often save a packet by buying from a specialist or motor factor (check your local *Yellow Pages*). Some cars were fitted with cats as an option before they became a legal requirement – in these cases, their performance isn't measured the same way at MoT time and, indeed, they can be replaced with conventional exhaust boxes. Any vehicles built after 1993 are stuck with the cat.

← **'How far to the next garage?' Camel Trophy competitors know just how important preventative maintenance is! (Nick Dimbleby)**

→ Discoverys are
historically prone to
steering box problems.
You can alleviate this to
some extent by checking
the reservoir level on
a regular basis and
making sure it never runs
anywhere near dry. Use
top quality fluid.

Diesel engines

Both the 200 and 300 Tdi units are suitably tough
for Land Rover installation, but there are still
points to keep an eye on. As with the petrol units,
they'll last longer and perform better with regular
oil changes, and, once again, a goodly supply of
50/50 mix coolant is essential. Both are prone to
snapping cam belts and as this often leads to a
completely wrecked engine it's not something to be
taken lightly. It should be changed at 60,000 mile
(96,500km) intervals, though cautious owners often
bite the bullet and knock 10,000 (16,100) off that
figure. If you've just bought yours and are unsure
when the belt was last changed (if ever), invest in a
new one. It's not an easy DIY fit so you'll be paying
labour as well, but balance the cost of having a new
belt fitted against that of a complete engine rebuild
and you'll soon see the reasoning.

   Servicing at a specialist garage isn't that expensive
and though service intervals are higher than the V8,
remember that you're saving with every visit to the
pumps and again by not having to contend with all
those ignition components.

Electrical equipment

Most of the electrical equipment, such as electric
windows, sunroof, central locking, etc, is fairly
conventional stuff. Faults are quite common
and are most likely due to component failure.
However, with any such item, always check the
obvious things, such as a blown fuse, wires come
adrift, and, of course, faulty earth connections.
Substitution is advisable before replacing a
component; for example, if an electric window
won't wind up or down and the fuse is OK, try
swapping the connections at the switch. If it
works on another switch, then the original switch
is at fault. If the original switch works a different
window, then component failure is indicated. This
sounds a bit involved, but it isn't really, especially
when you check out some of the replacement
prices. It's often feasible to get such parts from
specialist dismantlers at a massive saving over the
new part.

Transmission

Gearbox oil changes aren't as important as those
for the engine and it's quite enough to follow
the manufacturer's recommendations. You can
do most good simply by using the 'box properly
in day-to-day use, changing gear at the right
time and using low-ratio for heavy duty work
such as towing large loads and driving off the
tarmac. One thing which will soon land you with
a large invoice is using the manual differential
lock (where fitted) whilst the vehicle is on a
metalled road. You'll get axle wind-up very
quickly and if you indulge too often you'll soon
be replacing various drivetrain components.
The Discovery uses old-fashioned propshafts
which have several greasing points, front and
rear. Happily, you can get underneath without
raising the vehicle, so there's no excuse for not
doing it. Just about every Land Rover ever made
will have a permanent covering of oil around
the front/rear differentials, and the main and
transfer gearboxes. As long as this remains a
light covering, with the occasional drip onto the
driveway, there's no cause for concern. When
you find yourself swimming in a lake of EP80, it's
time to look more closely!

← Keep an eye on your tyre pressures and check your wheels regularly for signs of damage. There's a huge choice of second-hand alloy wheels, so check out the Land Rover magazines and your local specialist spares outlet (which often have postcard-type advert boards). These are the author's standard steel wheels plus **MT** tyres for getting around in the snowy Welsh mountains. Regardless, it's important to secure them properly to avoid theft.

↓ A cover for the rear wheel is always a good idea. It makes the back end look tidier, though this standard plastic Land Rover item is a bit simplistic and doesn't keep the tyre itself clean (so that would be messy at puncture time).

↑ Make sure you add a locking wheel bolt here because it's just so easy to attack on the rear door.

→ Far better is this sort of all-enclosing cover, which not only looks smarter and keeps the wheel and tyre clean but also gives you a chance to advertise your company! In addition, an opportunist thief has to guess whether or not it's worth getting involved here – is there an alloy wheel under there or not?

Neither the gearbox nor the transfer box lend themselves to DIY removal or repair – they're large lumps of metal and removal from underneath requires a large ramp and some specialist kit of the sort readily available at LEGS, who specialise in Land Rover 'boxes.

Steering

The Discovery steering box is known for leaking, but there's little you can do other than make sure it always has enough fluid in the reservoir. Check it when you check the coolant/oil/brake fluid levels and you should be OK. Look out for the first signs of uneven wear at the front tyres, which indicates some kind of misalignment, most probably tracking. Steering wheel shake as you drive over bumps could be the steering damper, but it could also be that the pre-load on the steering swivels needs adjusting. It's a DIY job as long as you've got some time, a spring balance, and a liking for working in bucket-loads of oil!

Suspension

The suspension is conventional, so needs only conventional checks. Look for signs of oil leaking from the dampers, and, having pressure-washed the underside of the car, look hard all around the springs for signs of cracking.

Tyres

Good tyres aren't cheap so regular inspection is worthwhile. Check the pressures at least weekly and adjust for the type of driving – long sessions of high-speed motorway work require higher pressures than playing in the mud. If you live in a rural area, where bad winter weather drastically affects the driving conditions, consider buying a set of deeper-treaded tyres on 'slave wheels' for winter-only use. The author uses road-biased tyres during the summer, on a set of stylish alloy wheels, with a set of MT (mud-terrain) tyres on standard steel wheels from November to March. (When it snows in the Welsh mountains, it really snows …) Of course, if you fancy going off-roading on a regular basis the same principle will apply.

Bodywork and chassis

Keeping the bodywork clean is a good move. Use a quality car shampoo (never washing-up liquid, which contains the enemy of paintwork, salt), and rinse off well. With gleaming bodywork you've an opportunity to check for any accident damage or signs of corrosion – the most common form this will take is electrolytic reaction where steel and alloy meet.

Invest in a pressure washer and keep the muck and crud from building up underneath. Get into all the nooks and crannies, especially during the winter months when road salt will eat through the steel panels and even the chassis in double-quick time. It pays also to get plenty of anti-corrosion liquids under there, something like Waxoyl or Dinitrol. Keep a weather eye on the sills and floor panels, particularly the front foot wells, which collect everything the front tyres throw back at them and regularly rot through.

Interior

As we've already seen, Discovery interiors got better over time, but have never been the best assembled or produced. Their fragility is just one of those things and all you can do is treat the inside carefully – easier said than done if you've a herd of unruly eight-year-olds to contend with. Seats and shelves can be repaired or replaced quite easily and cheaply by specialists such as Nationwide Trim. However, most of the plastic panels are Land Rover-only items, and unless you can find something suitable in a dismantlers you'll have to pay top dollar for replacements.

Security

Security is a big issue with any Discovery. Series 2 and 3 models came with a veritable armoury of anti-theft measures, but earlier cars were not so well defended. Any large Land Rover vehicle is a valuable prize to the thief because there's a huge market not only for stolen cars (which take on a new identity) but also for spares – remember that the engine, gearbox, and most of the running gear will also fit the Range Rover and Defender. A full description of security measures worth taking is given in Chapter Eight.

Buying spares

Spares from a Land Rover main agent aren't particularly expensive compared with some 4x4s, but they're even cheaper from the plethora of specialist concerns – check out the pages of the Land Rover magazines for details. In some cases, you can buy an original part in a different box and save lots of money, though in others, you'll be offered a selection of different quality items; by definition, buy the best you can afford, especially when it comes to safety-related products such as brakes, tyres, and suspension.

↖ ↙ **As Land Rover has moved ever more upmarket, it has left the way clear for knowledgeable specialists to sell both the cars themselves and a vast array of parts and accessories. In many cases the parts sold are the same as Land Rover originals but in different boxes. (Courtesy McDonald Land Rover Limited)**

CHAPTER 8
MODIFICATIONS

A sure sign that a vehicle has reached the heart of the 'enthusiast' is the number of modifications available. For the Discovery, the list is seemingly endless, the pages of the specialist magazines being awash with advertisements for companies who can supply products and services aimed at making your Discovery better in some way. These range from simple things like super-tough carpet mat sets and load protectors to complete engine and gearbox rebuilds. This chapter covers some of the more popular modifications.

It's a gas

It's long been one of the great Land Rover quandaries: you want the torque, power and offbeat rumble of that lusty V8, but the thought of feeding its petrol habit makes you quake in your boots. The answer is LPG – liquid petroleum gas. Convert your car to run on LPG (whilst retaining the petrol-power option) and you'll be running on almost half-price fuel. Better still, it's a 'clean' fuel in terms of exhaust emissions (see below), and because it burns so cleanly it's better for the engine, too; oil stays cleaner for longer and spark plugs look almost new after 10,000 miles (16,000km). Obviously, there's a cost to convert, but it's about a third of the cost to change the engine to a Tdi diesel unit, which makes plenty of sense when the LPG car will do the same – or more – mpg by price.

As a vehicle fuel, it's actually far safer than petrol. The gas is kept in a massively strong tank which is typically around four times thicker than the average fuel tank. Three solenoids within the system check for leakage and if one is detected, they instantly shut off the flow of gas. When filling, the gas is pumped in under pressure and so, unlike petrol, you can't get spillage all over the forecourt – and your shoes. The downside is that you have to find space for the LPG tank, but there's so much choice around nowadays

that there is bound to be something suitable for just about everyone.

It's important to find high quality equipment, designed specifically for your Discovery. Just as important is to have it installed correctly; using a true professional is probably cheaper in the long run, and he will also have the right equipment for setting up the system correctly – not something that can be done by guesswork.

EMISSIONS COMPARISONS
Compared to petrol, LPG typically produces:

- 75 per cent less carbon monoxide
- 85 per cent less hydrocarbons
- 40 per cent less oxides of nitrogen
- 87 per cent less ozone forming potential
- 10 per cent less carbon dioxide.

And compared to diesel, it produces:

- 90 per cent less particulates
- 90 per cent less oxides of nitrogen
- 70 per cent less ozone forming potential
- 60 per cent less carbon monoxide.

CONVERTING TO LPG
Converting a Discovery to run on LPG is perhaps not as difficult as you might imagine. The original petrol engine fuel injection components are retained, and a relatively small number of additional components need to be fitted to allow the engine to run on LPG as well as petrol.

← A large range of special equipment is available for serious off-road use. (Nick Dimbleby)

DID YOU KNOW?
Remember to consider your insurance company when modifying your car. Some have safety ramifications – suspension, for example. Whilst some are only cosmetic, if they're seen to increase the value or desirability of the vehicle your insurers could use them as a tool against you should it be stolen and you didn't tell them.

By far the largest of the LPG system components is the tank. There are many and various tank sizes and locations, so you have to decide which is best for your own use. Consider what you need to carry in the rear of the car; if you need the luggage space or regularly take passengers in the rear seats, you'll need to consider mounting the tank under the vehicle. You can have single or twin tanks fitted to brackets welded to the chassis, underneath the driver/passenger's feet. Or you can opt for a tank fitted in place of

the original, in-between the rear chassis legs. You could opt for one, or more usually two, under-sill tanks. These compromise ground clearance slightly and need to be fitted correctly to specially welded frames. If the rear luggage/people space isn't an issue, you can fit the tank on the load floor or, better still, fit two tanks, which still allow the seats to fold down.

The photos here were taken at RPi Engineering, V8 engine specialists and suppliers of Iwema LPG equipment. Their range of tanks is extensive and they have lots of experience in converting all manner of engines to LPG, from standard, carburetted 3.5-litres right up to S2 bored-out 5.3-litres.

With an LPG tank, because there can be no electrics within the tank, the 'fuel' gauge works magnetically and isn't awfully accurate. RPi use the sender information and connect it to a four-LED display in the cabin which 'counts down' from green to red as the fuel is used. A conventional dial/needle type gauge is an option.

If an LPG tank is fitted in place of the original petrol tank, it is necessary to add a separate

↘ **This is the basic Iwema componentry required for a standard LPG conversion to a fuel-injected Discovery. Two small black boxes (emulators) plug in between the fuel-injectors and the ECU. Without these, the ECU would shut everything down as the system switched from petrol to LPG.**

↓ **This LPG tank from RPi, which fits in place of the original petrol tank, comes with brackets which are fitted onto the chassis, enabling a neat fit.**

petrol tank. The tank used by RPi is a high-quality stainless steel unit, which fits rather neatly under the offside rear wing in such a way as to allow the original fuel filler neck to be utilised.

From the tank, the liquid LPG passes through a vaporiser, which turns it into a gas suitable for burning by the engine. The gas is then piped into the air-intake/plenum chamber via a mixer which is fitted in-line. The mixer size has to be balanced carefully with engine size/type and the vaporiser. Iwema technology means that mixers up to (currently) 50mm can be used.

LPG has an octane rating roughly equivalent of the old five-star petrol (are you that old?), so a better spark will help give more power and better economy. Make sure your plugs are a good brand and adjusted correctly. Using uprated HT leads will also help.

→ **For this LPG installation by RPi, a stainless-steel petrol tank is used …**

↓ **… which fits under the offside rear wing. This view is looking back at the tank from the position of the rear wheel (removed for installation).**

↓ This is the Eberspächer Hydronic pre-heater basic kit – minus the myriad of wires, connectors, and fasteners.

↑ The Hydronic system exhaust has to be routed clear of anything that could be affected by the heat it generates. Here, it was easy to take it straight down the inner wing, exiting below the vehicle.

↓ On this early V8, the Hydronic unit is mounted at the top of the offside wing, out of the way of rain and muck splashed up from below, and away from much of the engine heat.

Hot stuff

Yes, your Discovery already has a heater, but the Eberspächer unit does more than just keep your toes warm. Eberspächer is a name synonymous with vehicle heating, and for the Discovery enthusiast one of the company's Hydronic pre-heaters is well worth considering. The device works on petrol or diesel engines and fits in the engine bay, taking a tiny supply of fuel from the vehicle's tank. Working rather like a mini central heating system, it heats the vehicle's coolant, using a built-in pump to shift it around the engine. (Diesel versions also have a fuel pump.) There are several temperature safety devices to prevent it overheating, so you won't come out to find your pride and joy doing kettle impersonations.

Finding a location for the Hydronic unit itself is often the hardest part. Certainly, there is plenty of room under an early V8 bonnet, but later models with twin batteries, air conditioning, and all sorts of optional extras, may create more of a challenge.

Another important point to bear in mind is the routing of the Hydronic exhaust, which has to be routed away from anything that could be affected by the heat it generates.

It is controlled via a three-program, seven-day, mini timer which is surface-mounted on the dash or wherever is convenient. There's also an option of a remote control device (similar to an alarm 'plipper') which works at distances up to 75m (82yd) and enables the user to start the pre-heater from the comfort of the office or front room. It can be fitted instead of or as well as the mini timer. In terms of running costs, the Hydronic takes just 0.5l (0.1gal) per hour, and as it works from the vehicle's fuel system it can be used anywhere. If required, the heater fan can be connected to the unit so that if left switched on, it will blow hot air to the screen or car as required. A fully-fused relay is used to prevent the possibility of electrical problems.

There are several types of Hydronic system available, to suit both petrol and diesel-engined Range Rovers. The D4W is suitable for engines up to 2.5 litres, with the D5W being fitted to engines over that capacity.

↑ Racing Discoverys call for the ultimate modifications, not least in terms of safety. (Nick Dimbleby)

↑ **Compare these Rimmer Sports exhaust headers with the original cast-iron monstrosities above, and you'll see why the exhaust gas flow is much better.**

Exhausting

A stainless steel exhaust is a great investment if you're looking to keep your Discovery for any length of time, and there's not much price difference compared to the Land Rover official parts. Fitting an exhaust system can be done on a DIY basis, but it's well worth investing a few extra pounds and letting your local exhaust specialist do it for you; most of the fasteners will seize and few of us have recourse to oxyacetylene kit, which makes removal so much easier. And, of course, working with the car in the air on a four-post ramp hugely reduces the time of the job. Fitting a good sports exhaust system can provide much improved exhaust gas flow, leading to increased power and torque throughout the rev range.

Roof rack

Many Discoverys came with the original equipment roof rails with the very useful detachable crossbars (which were stored under the rear seat when not in use). However, these rails weren't made for really heavy use or carrying really big loads; for that, you need some good old-fashioned lumps of steel.

Towing the line

Adding a towbar to your Discovery makes it ready to do the job it's ideally suited for: towing. All Tdi and V8 models make great tow cars, being the right layout – a wheel almost right out at each corner – with plenty of torque to cope with most loads, and four-wheel drive. Because the car is legally able to pull such large loads, you're well-advised to go for the German-manufactured (Oris) factory-fit towbar, which has been specifically designed to cope with the massive stresses and strains towing places on it. Better still, it will fit easily into existing holes, which makes life easier.

Up the ladder to the roof

As we've seen, the Discovery is more than capable off-road and will take you trekking through jungles or deserts as you wish – check out the Camel Trophy models. However, whilst most of us won't actually do that, it's nice to imply that we could. Items such as a

THE BENEFITS OF BEING WARM

Starting your car with a warm engine greatly reduces wear on its internal parts – some 75 per cent of engine wear occurs in the first ten minutes as all that excess fuel required washes the oil off the bores. It means you start with no choke (or extra fuel from the injection system) so you save fuel, which in turn saves both the planet and your wallet. If your Discovery is a later model with a catalyst exhaust, you'll benefit because the warmer the cat, the more efficient it is. The interior heater will work straight away and so warm the car and clear a frosty screen quickly.

And in *really* cold weather (oddly enough, becoming more common in the UK as global warming takes hold), a standard engine will often not produce enough heat for the heater to work efficiently, leading in turn to misted windows. When this is the case, the Hydronic unit can be turned on manually whilst on the move to add a welcome warm boost. More importantly, it will be a comfort to anyone using their Discovery in one of the more remote parts of the country, where winters are harsher; as the Hydronic can be used to heat the car in the event of a snowy breakdown, miles from anywhere, it could literally be a life saver.

rear-mounted ladder help convey that impression to drivers of lesser vehicles. Of course, it could also be used to help get equipment onto the roof rack.

Side-stepping the height

Side steps are another popular accessory fitment. They are seen by some as merely improving the looks, although they are a genuine boon to the elderly, the infirm, and those who are a little short of leg. But remember that they drastically reduce the ground-clearance, meaning that serious off-roading is now off-limits, and that when driving in snow or mud the car will ground much earlier.

↙ The Oris towbar kit contains everything you need to complete the job – except a few spanners. There's even a sachet of grease for the towball.

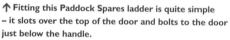

↑ Fitting this Paddock Spares ladder is quite simple – it slots over the top of the door and bolts to the door just below the handle.

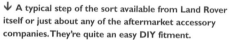

↓ A typical step of the sort available from Land Rover itself or just about any of the aftermarket accessory companies. They're quite an easy DIY fitment.

→ Modifying your Discovery to Camel Trophy spec is possible – but hugely expensive. (Nick Dimbleby)

DID YOU KNOW?

As a rule, don't expect your modifications to make much impact on the resale price. More comprehensive changes, such as LPG or diesel conversions, can change the value, but such things as fog lamps, roof racks, and alloy wheels will usually just add to its desirability in a market where there really is a lot of choice.

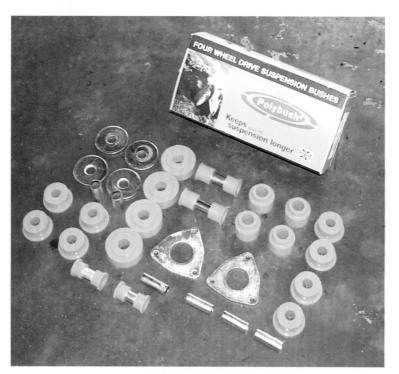

them at ten years old – no wonder they wander. Polybushes tighten up the ride very effectively and make it possible to judge accurately the state of the other suspension components. If you haven't got anti-roll bars (front and rear) then that's the next logical step. There are various manufacturers of proprietary kits, as well as Land Rover's own. All will need fixing plates welding to the front and rear axles, so unless you're a real wizard welder it's a job for the professionals, not least because of the accuracy required. Choosing the right dampers and springs requires some input from a professional who knows the business; the 'right' equipment for the enthusiast off-roader is unlikely to be the right choice for motorway-man.

Replacing springs and dampers is a fairly simple DIY job as long as you've sufficient heavy duty kit at hand, notably a high-quality trolley jack/axle stands and a tough 1/2" driver (at least) socket set, capable of shifting fastenings which will doubtless be somewhat recalcitrant.

↑ **These orange versions of the classic bush were produced specially for Scorpion racing, to match their own anti-roll bar dampers and springs.**

Doing up the dash

There's no doubt that a touch of wood in the cabin adds a touch of flash to the dash (note how it's been used to take the Range Rover into Jaguar and Mercedes territory). You can upgrade your Discovery by fitting a kit like this from the accurately named Walnut Dash Company. Each kit is a self-adhesive precision-cut walnut trim and there's a kit for each Discovery model (complete with ten-year warranty), and it's so easy to fit.

Rock and roll

The Discovery is a tall, heavy vehicle which demands much of the suspension components. Few handle at all well in standard form, least of all those cars not fitted with anti-roll bars. Uprating the suspension is sufficiently popular for there to be a huge choice available, which is a double-edged sword; on the one hand, the prices are kept down; on the other, it's very easy for the uninformed owner to inadvertently make the wrong choice.

The best advice is to start with the basics and almost any Discovery much over four years old will benefit from the fitment of polyurethane bushes in place of the rubber originals. Even at that stage they will be worn, and many Discoverys still sport

FITTING POLYBUSHES

This isn't really a DIY job unless you've got access to lots of expensive equipment. Though some of the original bushes wouldn't be too difficult to sort, some of the securing bolts will undoubtedly be very reluctant to leave home. The torque required can be extreme and impossible to apply with the vehicle simply jacked up on the ground. Polybush sets usually come in two types, a classic somewhat harder bush, coloured red, and a slightly softer 'comfort' bush, coloured blue.

FITTING ANTI-ROLL BARS

There are various anti-roll bars to choose from. Scorpion Racing uses its own bars, which are much thicker than those furnished by Land Rover but use the original Land Rover axle fitting kit.

In essence the fitting is not difficult, though many of the fasteners will have rusted solid and will require a great deal of torque to remove them. This requires high-quality tools and the wherewithal to lift the car safely off the ground – if you don't have both, go to a professional. This applies even more so when it comes to the welding of the brackets to the axles' casings. They have to be fitted in exactly the right position and seam-welded for strength – not a job to practise on.

→ **Here you can see a direct comparison between Polybushes and the original (at top right). Note that the new bushes are in two halves, which is one reason why they're so easy to fit.**

↑ A Scorpion Racing front anti-roll bar, not only looks pretty in Scorpion orange but massively improves the ride quality of the car.

← It's a similar story at the rear. The front mounting of the anti-roll bar is bolted into place and the rear mounting is welded to the axle casing.

↓ A set of Scorpion Racing dampers and springs ready to be fitted to a lucky Discovery.

FITTING UPRATED SPRINGS AND DAMPERS

Fitting dampers and springs is within the reach of most keen DIY Discovery owners and decent products are not difficult to find. According to Colin Aldred of Scorpion, a common mistake is for owners to fit the heavy-duty springs at the front and the others at the rear. The result of this is that the car not only looks ridiculous, with a massive nose-up stance, but handles dreadfully. Remember that most of the weight is generated at the rear of the vehicle, especially when loaded-up or towing.

Obviously, you need to think about whether your Discovery is going to spend most of its time on- or off-road, as this will influence your choice of springs and dampers. Fitting at the rear is easier than the front, because at the rear the dampers and springs are separate, and there are no engine-bay components to get in the way. However, if you've an anti-roll bar, it may have to be released to allow sufficient axle movement with the new suspension components.

FITTING A MAD INTERACTIVE SUSPENSION

Retro-fit airbags? Yes, but perhaps not as you might think, because the MAD bags (a Dutch system imported into the UK) are actually incredibly tough

polyurethane units which fit inside the rear coil springs. They don't interfere with the normal running of the car but are enormously useful when there's lots of weight to be carried or towed.

Air pressure is added to compensate for the extra stresses and strains applied when carrying heavy loads or when towing. This works to great effect and gets rid of that tail-heavy attitude which can lead to steering, braking, lighting, and general handling problems. When not required, the air pressure is released and the suspension reverts to standard.

Normally the bags would be topped up using a small compressor or a garage air line, but if you want you can opt for an on-board compressor, permanently linked to the airbag system. This makes

↑ A completed MAD interactive suspension unit is shown here in situ.

← This is the basic MAD set-up, comprising air bags, tough polyurethane spacers, and the plastic tube which connects the airbags to the supply.

it much more versatile, allowing you to make your suspension hard or soft as you like, whenever you like. The built-in gauge shows the state of play at all times. In 'normal' cars it would usually be mounted under the vehicle with a remote switch in the cabin. However, with the world's best off-roader, it's usually best to mount it inside! The device automatically checks the pressure and pumps it to the minimum should it drop too low. A heat shield is always fitted to prevent heat from the exhaust affecting the airbags.

In-car entertainment (ICE)

Many owners will want to upgrade the head unit as supplied by Land Rover. However, the standard plug is specific to the car, which means it won't connect directly into the back of a modern head unit, most of which have standardised Euro-style DIN connections. But by using a simple adaptor from Autoleads you can link the new deck to the original wiring without the need for cutting and shutting – which also means you can re-install the original deck easily when it comes to resale time.

Security

Whether your Discovery is heavily-modded or totally standard, it's a tasty prize for the thief. Because of the way that Land Rover products can be pulled apart and their components interchanged, they're highly prized. Equally, many of them find their way to foreign markets. Over the years, standard-fit immobilisers became common and, latterly, compulsory – Series 2 cars in particular have much-improved security systems. Depending on the model, an integrated alarm may also have been fitted. If you've no security, then an immobiliser is the least you can do. Fit an alarm with it for more peace of mind, and when you link it into your electric windows and central locking you'll have the convenience of single button locking/alarming together with a screaming siren to warn of intruders.

THATCHAM
Based at Thatcham in Berks, this is the insurance industry's testing body. Security devices are submitted by the manufacturers and undergo many harsh tests to ensure that they are of the highest quality. This includes moisture and vibration tests

↓ A Thatcham alarm/ immobiliser, such as this top-level, digital Clifford unit, can be hidden anywhere in the car. The system has to be installed by a professional, but check out all that wiring – would you want to attempt it?

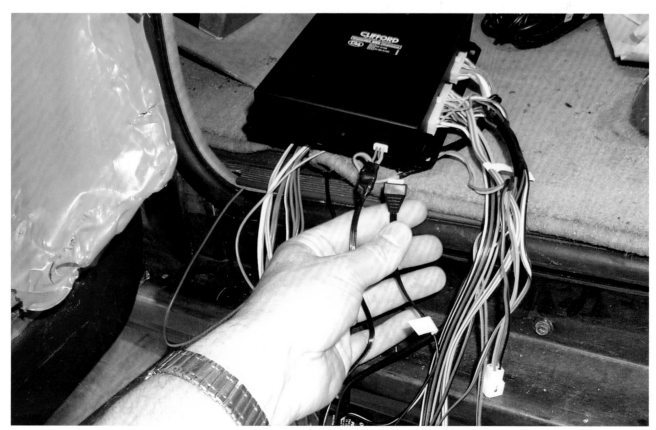

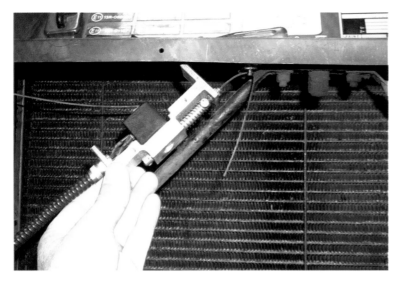

↑ The Carsafe bonnet protection device can be fitted into the existing release cable and ensures that the bonnet cannot be opened unless the ignition is 'on' and, where fitted, the security system has been disarmed.

→ These locking wheel bolts are designed for alloy wheels. Don't forget to secure the spare, too.

and resistance to physical attack. Thatcham has three categories, defined as follows:

Category 1
Combined alarm/immobiliser: Alarm with full perimetric and volumetric detection, and standby power supply. Immobiliser isolating a minimum of two circuits, passively armed. Anti-scan, anti-grab resistance of codes.

Category 2
Electronic/Electromechanical immobiliser: Immobiliser isolating a minimum of two circuits, passively armed. Anti-scan, anti-grab resistance of codes.

Category 2>1
Electronic/Electromechanical immobiliser: Immobiliser as Category 2 but which can easily be upgraded to Category 1 specification.

Category 3
Mechanical immobiliser: Immobiliser isolating a minimum of one operating system. Easy to arm and disarm. Attack resistant for five minutes minimum using a comprehensive range of hand tools. Can be permanently fitted, or temporarily DIY (temporary DIY mechanical immobilisers are listed as devices intended as supplementary security or security appropriate to lower risk vehicles).

Category Q
An unusual category in that products are not actually approved as such, but are tested by the organisation and a report issued as a result. Tracking devices are typically found in this category.

INSURANCE DISCOUNTS
The fitting of a Thatcham Category 1 or 2 device will, in many cases, bring with it an insurance discount (and/or a lowering of theft excess, etc). However, it is important that you check with your insurers before fitting the product; discounting remains somewhat muddled, and not all companies offer the same discounts and terms. Moreover, any discount available has to be related to the gross figure, and shopping around remains as important as ever.

One important aspect for Category 1 and 2 products is that they must be installed professionally and an official certificate of installation obtained as proof for the insurers. A full list of the latest approved Thatcham products can be obtained by sending a large SAE to: Department VS, Association of British Insurers, 51 Gresham Street, London, EC2V 7HQ. If you're computer literate, there's a complete listing in PDF format on the web site at www. thatcham.org.

UNDERBONNET SECURITY
Another very weak point on the Discovery is the vulnerability of the bonnet; it can easily be opened by a clued-up thief, giving access to an alarm siren, immobilisation circuits, and the battery. The Carsafe is fitted into the existing release cable and the internal solenoid ensures that the bonnet cannot be opened unless the ignition is 'on' and, where fitted, the security system has been disarmed.

WHEELS
One of the easiest targets on any Discovery is the wheels and tyres. Alloy or steel, they've all got a

value, especially if the tyres are a bit special. Use locking wheel bolts, but make sure you get the right type – different bolts should be used for steel and alloy wheels. Don't forget to secure the spare, too, as that's got to be easiest of all to steal.

THE TRUE COSTS

The true cost of having your Discovery stolen is far more than you would at first imagine. Firstly, there's the inconvenience of having no vehicle – taking public transport is expensive and awkward, hiring a car is incredibly expensive. And as a car is only 'stolen not recovered' after 30 days, that's a whole month's inconvenience to start with. Then there's the haggling with your insurers over the value of the vehicle. This can be protracted and almost always leaves a deficit to be made up by the owner in order to replace the vehicle with one of equal standing.

The excess – the first amount of any claim paid by the insured – can be as low as £50, but is usually much more than that, and in some cases as much as £500. Then there's the matter of no-claims discount (NCD). Most companies set the insured back two years NCD for a claim, usually 20 per cent. Add one-fifth to your last year's gross premium to see how much difference that would

make. And don't forget that whilst you go back 20 per cent, you only go forward 10 per cent per year, so you're penalised for two years. In addition, the insurers could impose special terms if they feel the circumstances of the claim demanded it.

For drivers with a suitable driving history, it is often possible to 'protect' the NCD. However, insurers are always at liberty to refuse to offer reinsurance to anyone they feel is an unacceptable risk, and any other insurer will penalise you for your claims history. All this is expensive and inconvenient and is the reason why you should secure your Discovery – now!

BASIC RULES

- Park sensibly – down a dark alley is asking for trouble.
- Don't leave valuables in the car, especially credit cards, cheque books, etc.
- If you've installed an alarm, use it! It's surprising how many people don't.
- If you must leave anything in the car, put it out of sight.
- Lock your Discovery whenever you leave it, even in the garage.
- Don't relax at home; a huge proportion of thefts occur at or near the owners' homes.

← Shown here undergoing an attack test, the Autolok fits over the steering wheel and is an effective and highly visible deterrent to would-be car thieves.

CHAPTER 9
COMPETITION – THE CAMEL TROPHY

Let's really off-road!

In terms of conventional motor sport, you're unlikely to find Discoverys taking part in saloon car racing or rallying (although there's likely to be quite a few in the car park, there as towing vehicles). However, Land Rover has a long association with the world-famous Camel Trophy event. When this competition was instigated in 1980 Jeeps were the chosen vehicles, but from 1981 Land Rover provided the vehicles used by the competitors, the aim being to put hand-picked teams from all over the world through some of the most arduous conditions imaginable; crossing swollen rivers (after having built a bridge first), navigating through miles of dense jungle, and participating in special stages designed to test men (and women, who first took part in 1994) and machines to their limits. The Discovery was first used in 1990 in three-door Tdi guise, after which five-door Tdi models were used up to 1997, at which point Land Rover's marketing team switched to the then-new Freelander. The final Camel Trophy was held in 2000, but Land Rover is said to be contemplating starting its own similar event. One can only hope.

The object, from Land Rover's point of view, was simple: to show the buying public that the Discovery was as rough and tough as any vehicle in the line-up and that, despite its more mainstream image, it could easily mix it off-road with the likes of the Defender and Range Rover. It certainly worked well, and made the specially-prepared Camel Trophy Discoverys sought-after in their own right. They are distinctive vehicles, finished in 'sandglow' – a colour chosen to mimic the corporate colour of the Camel logo – and simply dripping with serious off-road equipment. (The rather startling orange/yellow hue of the Camel Discoverys is actually an official British Leyland colour from way back in the mists of time, its official part number being STC1489/A, colour code LRC361.)

Not surprisingly, many owners make their own 'copies' of Camel Trophy vehicles, which is fine as long as they're not being sold as originals. In line with Land Rover's more aggressive marketing policies of late, there's also a plethora of Camel-badged gear to buy, from seriously chunky boots to wristwatches and the ubiquitous baseball caps. Although the winners' trophy came to the UK in 1989 (when the competition was held in the Amazon and Bob and Joe Ives won in a Land Rover 110), no British team has ever won it in a Discovery.

What was the Camel Trophy?

To even the most enthusiastic off-roader, competing in the Camel Trophy sounds like some sort of insane jail sentence. For around three weeks you take your fully-equipped vehicle for over 1,000 miles (1,600km) through dense and dangerous jungles, disease-ridden swamps, and along unmade mountain tracks with sheer drops at every corner; and now and then you find yourself having to chop down the odd tree and lash bits of it together to create a makeshift bridge to cross a raging river. It was never an individual event, each country sending a team which had to work as an efficient unit in order to survive. And whilst working as a team gained you extra points, if you worked to help an opposing team, you got still more! It hardly sounds the sort of thing you'd do for fun, but an incredible one million applicants a year put their names in the hat for a chance to be one of just 80 people (40 teams of two) chosen.

← As if the Camel Trophy wasn't hard enough, later events included seperate kayaking and mountain-biking stages. (Nick Dimbleby)

> **DID YOU KNOW?**
> To capitalise on the publicity generated by the Camel Trophy, special edition Discoverys were launched in both Japan and Germany..

↑ Not surprisingly, there's an enthusiastic club for fans and owners of Camel Trophy vehicles. This shows an excellent example on their stand at one of the many Land Rover events.

A brief history of the Camel Trophy

When first staged in 1980 it was distinctly low-profile. Three German teams loaded up a collection of CJ6 Jeeps and headed off to the Transamazonica Highway in South America for some modern-day adventuring. Somewhere, somehow, someone sat up and took notice, deciding that this wasn't half a bad idea, especially if your company produced vehicles which claimed to be the toughest 4x4s in the world. What better way to prove it? The following year, the event was staged in Sumatra and Land Rover supplied all the competing vehicles – V8 Range Rovers. From 1981 until 1998 (the last year that Discoverys were used), Land Rover continued to make the event its own, its marketing department hanging on to all the publicity potential available.

Unlike a normal rally, or even something like the Paris–Dakar, the Camel Trophy was never a race, more a test of endurance. Throughout the route, the organisers would introduce what were effectively special stages, which could be a winching test or, in later events, mountain biking or even kayaking.

Environmental pressure groups have criticised the event for trampling around with impunity in areas that should be left to nature. However, such folk know little of the event and the effort that was taken to ensure that no environmental damage was done. In fact, some of the projects set for the teams have been positively beneficial to the local people, by clearing overgrown jungle tracks, or repairing bridges that the authorities were not able to. As such, the event often left a really positive impact behind it once it had finished.

And the name …

Most folk think, quite naturally, that the Trophy got its name from the Camel cigarette brand. Well, that's sort of right, inasmuch as the actual trademark is the property of Worldwide Brands International (WBI). This is part of the RJR Nabisco corporation, which in turn owns Camel Cigarettes. But still ciggies aren't involved, because in 1977 WBI in Germany started a brand of leisurewear with the Camel logo on it and it was this that became the sponsor of the Trophy. As the event grew, so did the leisurewear company, and there's a whole stack of stuff for the enthusiast to buy, including boots, caps, watches, coats, and fleeces. From 1992–8 the event was co-sponsored by Land Rover, who also made plenty of marketing headway from the kudos associated with it.

The vehicles

The cars themselves were pulled off the production line for some very special treatment by Land Rover's Special Vehicles Division. In preparing them, the company had to make them safe and able to cope with the incredibly arduous

Year	Destination	Approx (km)	Winning country	Model
1990	Siberia	1,500	Netherlands	200 Tdi 3-door
1991	Tanzania–Burundi	1,600	Turkey	200 Tdi 5-door
1992	Guyana	1,600	Switzerland	200 Tdi 5-door
1993	Sabah, Malaysia	1,500	USA	200 Tdi 5-door
1994	Argentina–Paraguay–Chile	2,590	Spain	200 Tdi 5-door
1995	Mundo-Maya	1,700	Czech Republic	300 Tdi 5-door
1996	Kalimantan	1,850	Greece	300 Tdi 5-door
1997	Mongolia	1,500	Austria	300 Tdi 5-door

↓ **A correctly adorned roof rack (genuine, because it bolts through the bodywork into the internal roll cage) complete with all the toys – Hella Rallye 1000 lamps, sand ladders, etc.**

DID YOU KNOW?

Not all ex-Camel Trophy Discoverys reached the open market. Apart from those which didn't make it back in one piece, many were used as training vehicles for the following year's event.

↑ **Crossing bridges in a Camel Discovery is easy; first build your bridge ...** (Nick Dimbleby)

conditions, but at the same time use mostly components that were readily available and not too specialised. The aim was to ensure that they would still be running happily at the end of three weeks of the harshest treatment known to man; there aren't many Land Rover dealers in the middle of the jungle. Attention was paid to protecting the occupants (using super-strong Safety Devices roll cages, fire extinguishers, etc), and vulnerable mechanical components such as the steering and axles.

Buying your own Camel Trophy Discovery

It's given to few of us to take part in the event itself (most of us wouldn't get more than a few kilometres anyway!) but you can still own your own Camel Trophy Discovery. By definition, there were never many official cars produced and fewer still were actually sold on the open market. As such any car offered as a Camel Trophy vehicle should be approached with much circumspection. There are

plenty of checks to carry out but by far the best advice is to contact the Camel Trophy Owners Club (see Appendix), who will be able to steer you clear of buying a duffer. A very important point to consider is the mileage; don't cut down on pre-buying checks just because it's not travelled very far – if it's a genuine Camel, it probably won't have done. But think about how hard it's had to work in that relatively short distance; having travelled up mountains, through swamps, and up to its bonnet in raging rivers will put years on any car.

For some, only a totally original competition car will do the job, regardless of how hard it's had to work. But there's another way, and that's to consider a Marshal's car – by normal standards they'll still have had a hard time, but in Camel terms they'll have had a stroll in the park. They're usually recognisable by

↑ Would you let these men work on your car? Camel Trophy entrants have to be able to do the odd 'running repair'! (Nick Dimbleby)

DID YOU KNOW?

Though it was used for eight years in the Camel Trophy, the Discovery was never powered by the V8 petrol engine.

the communications kit they have, such as the aerial bracket on the rear three-quarter panel.

By definition again, Camel vehicles have had rather more to put up with than your average Discovery – cracked bulkheads, for example, are common, caused through having one too many heavy landings. And as has already been seen, the Camel cars were prone to spending much of their time in the water, which will have an obvious effect just about everywhere – in the engine bay, and particularly on the interior. Bumps, lumps, and scrapes abound and an original one that hasn't been patched, filled, or sprayed a little is going to be rare.

Of course, there are plenty of 'replicas' around, packed to the hilt with off-road accessories and painted in the Camel colours. Many of these are excellent cars and there's nothing wrong with buying a good one, as long as they are sold as replicas, not the real thing, and at a suitably lower price. Another alternative is to create your own, but you'll need a really large wallet to do so because all those accessories are top quality items and are very expensive!

Camel-spotting

Approximately 400 real Camel Discoverys were produced, but remember that not all have appeared on the open market. Indeed, many were wrecked on the event. They come in both right-hand drive and left-hand drive, and with 200 and 300 series Tdi engines.

What follows are a few pointers to finding a genuine Camel Trophy Discovery; but remember, just as it's possible for a standard Discovery to be tricked-up to look like a Camel, it's possible for a Camel to have been changed over the years. All genuine cars were registered by Land Rover itself, so they have (or had originally – a cherished plate is always a possibility) a 'Birmingham' suffix, which will be: –AB, –AC, –DU, –JW, –KV, –ON, –OP, or –RW.

The Camel Trophy colour is readily available which means anyone can get to it with a spray gun and create a 'replica'. But check the logbook (V5), because its colour will be listed there as N/A (not available).

← **Just another day pulling a two-tonne Discovery up a vertical slope ... (Nick Dimbleby)**

→ **With more candlepower than Yorkshire, there's no excuse for hitting anything in the dark. (Nick Dimbleby)**

→ 'Typical! You travel 1,000 miles to find the beach, and there's not a deckchair attendant in sight!' (Nick Dimbleby)

↑ **Camel Trophy
Discoverys leaving the
Land Rover factory for
Mundo Maya in 1995.
This is the cleanest
they'll be for over 1,000
miles – or ever!**

At the front, the first thing to catch your eye should be a Huskey Superwinch, a special version for the event giving around 10,500lb (4,700kg) of pulling power. It's an electric unit so flipping open the bonnet should reveal a pair of batteries to help cope with the extra drain. And while you're there, the bonnet itself should have rally-style, quick-release pins in case it needs to be opened in a hurry – always a possibility on Camel Trophy jaunts. The bull bar was a necessity for the job in hand and on genuine cars it should have two metal loops at its top outer edges. These were for connecting the steel wires from there to the roof rack, the object being to deflect large lumps of jungle attacking the windscreen – not much use calling Auto Windscreens in the middle of South America!

At the rear of the bonnet, there should be a huge Mantec snorkel-style air intake, which enables the engine to breathe air rather than water when vehicles encountered deep water – and they often did.

Up on top, Camels had a serious roof rack, with a large rail to keep everything in place – everything, that is, including the sand ladders (four), pickaxe, shovels, four huge Hella Rallye 1000 work lamps at the front (and one at the rear), and a rear-door ladder. With the real thing, the rack bolts down through the roof directly into the internal Safety Devices roll cage. Aftermarket items generally fit to the roof gutter.

→ **'Who says a two-
tonne Camel Discovery
won't float?' River
crossing is easy with the
optional heavy-duty raft!
(Nick Dimbleby)**

Inside the car, all Camels were fitted with a Safety Devices roll cage, and in the rear a false floor was installed so that the recovery equipment could be stored underneath. Not surprisingly, the standard-issue radio/cassette deck wasn't much use on the Camel Trophy, so it was ditched in favour of a voltmeter.

Look underneath at the springs. At the front, original factory springs were fitted, but because of all the weight carried the rear springs actually had second so-called 'helper' springs within the standard units. Wheels are easy to swap and change and aren't that much of a pointer to originality – most come on conventional steels (often painted to match the body colour) and by definition, tyres wear out and have to be replaced. To cope with the massive stresses and strains placed upon them, the Camel Discoverys were fitted with uprated halfshafts with 24 splines. Dismantling bits of the car isn't necessary to check this; remove the plastic cover from the end of the rear halfshaft and you should be able to see the letters 'HD' stamped therein (indicating heavy-duty).

These pointers should be used as basic guidelines not so much to buying the car, but to stop you wasting your time on one which is obviously not what it purports to be. If you're reasonably satisfied that you are looking at a genuine Camel Discovery, then there's no doubt that you shouldn't really consider parting with your hard-earned cash until you've consulted the club. And, of course, it's possible that club members may have suitable vehicles for sale anyway.

APPENDIX
USEFUL CONTACTS AND SPECIFICATIONS

As well as the conventional address and telephone number for each company, e-mail and website addresses have also been included where available. If you are buying online, it is important to ensure that the site is 'secure' and that your credit card details cannot be stolen by a third party. In addition, we would not recommend any internet connection or e-mail communication without some form of anti-virus protection to inhibit potentially dangerous computer bugs getting into your system and wreaking havoc. A personal 'firewall' should prevent computer hackers breaking and entering your machine and stealing card and PIN numbers, etc. All addresses and sites were correct at the time of writing but are subject to change.

Autoleads Unit 80, Woolmer Trading Estate, Bordon, Hants, GU35 9QF. Tel: 01420 476767. E-mail: info@armourauto.com. Website: www.autoleads. co.uk. All manner of ICE accessories and adaptors to make connecting new items of sound equipment easy.

Brightwells Country Vehicle Auctions Easters Court, Leominster, Herefs, HR6 0DE. Tel: 01568 611325. E-mail: vehicles@brightwells.com. Website: www.brightwells.com. Auctioneers with a regular 4x4 auction which often includes around 100 Discoverys.

Burlen Fuel Systems Limited Spitfire House, Castle Road, Salisbury, Wilts, SP1 3SB. Tel: 01722 412500. E-mail: info@burlen.co.uk. Website: www. burlen.co.uk. SU carburettor sales and spares, as fitted to early V8 Discoverys.

Carflow. See Evo.

Clarke International Hemnal Street, Epping, Essex, CM16 4LG. Tel: 01992 565333. E-mail: sales@clarkeinternational.com. Website: www. clarkeinternational.com. All kinds of hand tools, pneumatic machinery and tools, work benches, etc.

Department of Transport Public Enquiries Unit. Tel: 0207 944 8300. All matters relating to vehicle/roads legislation and the environment. Website: www.dft.gov.uk.

Eberspächer (UK) Ltd Headlands Business Park, Salisbury Road, Ringwood, Hants, BH24 3PB. Tel: 01425 480151. E-mail: enquiries@ eberspacher.com. Website: www.eberspacher.com. Manufacturers of diesel and petrol engine vehicle heating systems including the Hydronic pre-heater, ideal for Discovery V8 or diesel engines.

Evo Automotive Solutions Unit 7, Denbigh Hall Industrial Estate, Bletchley, MK3 7QT. Tel: 01908 646566. Suppliers of top-quality Evo/ Carflow locking wheel bolts to suit Discovery steel or alloy wheels.

Jeremy J. Fearn Fold Farm, Beeley (Nr Matlock), Derbyshire, DE4 2NQ. Tel: 01629 732546. E-mail: jjf.interoolers@btinternet.com. Website: www.jeremyjfearn.co.uk. Diesel specialist supplying and fitting chip uprates and larger intercoolers for increased power, torque, and mpg.

Goodyear Great Britain Ltd TyreFort, 88-98 Wingfoot Way, Erdington, Birmingham B24 9HY. Tel: 0121 306 6000. Website: www.goodyear.co.uk. Wide range of quality on-road/off-road/in-between tyres designed specifically for the Discovery, fitted on some models as standard.

Gordon Finlay Woolcombes, Newton Poppleford, Sidmouth, Devon, EX10 0DF. Tel: 01395 567046. Website: www.gordonfinlay-lpgconversions.co.uk. LPG installation expert, supply and installation service of Iwema equipment.

Holley Carburettors See RPi Engineering.

Iwema Enterprise Hallenweg 0, 5615 PP, Eindhoven, Holland. Tel: 0(031) 40 252 3950. E-mail: info@iwemalpg.com. Website: www. iwemaenterprise.com. LPG conversion specialists, with a wide range of kits and components for all Discovery models including diesel. Producers of a very useful handbook of LPG installation. (See also RPi Engineering and Gordon Finlay.)

Kenlowe Limited Burchetts Green, Maidenhead, Berks, SL6 6QU. Tel: 01628 823303. E-mail: sales@ kenlowe.com. Website: www.kenlowe.com. Electric fan kits to replace original viscous version and Hot Start warm up device, both designed to aid efficiency and improve mpg.

Landcraft (David Mitchell's) Plas Yn Dre, High Street, Bala, Gwynedd, LL23 7LU. Tel: 01678 520820. Email: info@landcraft4x4.co.uk. Website: www. landcraft4x4.co.uk. Off-road courses in the beautiful Welsh mountains, off-road training, and a huge range of 4x4 models.

Land Rover Limited Land Rover UK, Banbury Road, Gaydon, Warwickshire, CV35 0RR. Website: www.landrover.com.

LEGS Unit 11 Canal Wood Industrial Estate, Chirk, Nr Wrexham, Clwyd, LL14 5RL. Tel: 01691 770044. E-mail: sales@legs.co.uk. Website: www.legs.co.uk. Manual transmission specialist reconditioners, including gearboxes, transfer boxes, and differentials, plus engines. Parts and mail order service.

MAD Suspension Comptek Limited, Unit 7 RO24 Twizel Close, Stonebridge, Milton Keynes, MK13 0DX. Tel: 01908 220308. E-mail: info@mad-suspension.com. Website: www.mad-suspension. co.uk. The interactive suspension 'airbag' system which uses a pneumatic pump to raise and lower rear springs to compensate for extra loads and/or large trailer weights. Ideal for those who regularly tow trailers.

McDonald Landrover Limited Unit 18, Mile Oak Industrial Estate, Oswestry, Shropshire, SY10 8GA. Tel: 01691 657705. Website: www. mcdonaldlandrover.co.uk. Spares, accessories, service, LPG fitting, and just about everything for the Land Rover/Discovery enthusiast.

McGard Website: www.mcgard.com. Manufacturers of excellent quality, award-winning Ultra High Security locking wheel nuts suitable for both alloy and steel wheels. Available from stockists.

Mr Fast'ner M&P Direct, Phoenix Way, Garngoch Industrial Estate, Gorseinon, Swansea, SA4 9HN. Tel: 0871 222 1122. E-mail: sales@mr-fastner.com. Website: www.mr-fastner.com. Suppliers of all types of fastener and Recoil thread repair kits, as well as polishing kits, tools, taps and dies, and other useful items for the Discovery owner.

Nationwide Trim Unit 17, West Washford Industrial Estate, Redditch, Worcs, B98 0DG. Tel: 01527 518851. Website: www.nationwidetrim. demon.co.uk/. Suppliers of all items of Discovery trim from a door panel to a complete refurbishment, as featured in the 'interiors' section of this book.

Paddock Spares and Accessories The Showground, The Cliff, Matlock, Derbyshire, ED4 5EW. Tel: 08454 584499. E-mail: sales@ paddockspares.com. Website: www.paddockspares. com. Mail-order service offering all manner of spares, accessories, and maintenance items to keep your Discovery happy without spending a fortune.

Pharmhouse Marketing (Mark Adams) Tel: 01694 720144, mobile 07798 582390. E-mail: mark.adams@pharmhouse.co.uk. An independent specialist working only with Rover V8 engine management, fuel injection, and ignition systems. New, remanufactured, and used parts, standard or uprated. Support for vehicles with catalytic converters by Lambda Correction Analysis. Computerised four-wheel drive rolling roads and engine dynamometer available to set-up and diagnose any vehicle.

Polybush Ltd Clywedog Road South, Wrexham Industrial Estate, Wrexham, LL13 9XS. Tel: 01978 664316. E-mail: sales@polybush.co.uk. Website: www.polybush.co.uk. Long-lasting and easy-to-fit Polybush polyurethane suspension bushes (dampers, anti-roll bar, Panhard rod, etc), in 'softer' standard format and original 'harder' classic versions.

Rimmer Brothers Limited Triumph House, Sleaford Road, Bracebridge Heath, Lincoln, LN4 2NA. Tel: 01522 568000. E-mail: sales@rimmerbros.co.uk. Website: www.rimmerbros.co.uk. Complete range of Discovery products from engines to wheel bolts, including their famous standard/sports stainless steel exhaust systems. Comprehensive free catalogue available.

RPi Engineering Wayside Garage, Holt Road, Horsford, Norwich, Norfolk, NR10 3EE. Tel: 01603 891209. Website: www.v8engines.com. Rover V8 engine specialists, rebuilding to original specification, tuned, or new capacity. Also custom-designed, high-tech V8 LPG conversions to exacting standards. Valuable contributors to this book and the fount of all Rover V8 knowledge.

Scorpion Racing Unit D, The Coppetts Centre, North Circular Road, London, N12 0SH. Tel: 0208 221 4888. E-mail: info@scorpion-racing.co.uk. Website: www.scorpion-racing.co.uk. Uprated dampers and springs by Decarbon to suit all types of Discovery requirements. The company also produces its own anti-roll bar system for retro-fitting or upgrading and markets its suspension Polybushes with its own orange colouring.

SIP (Industrial Products Ltd) Gelders Hall Road, Shepshed, Loughborough, Leics, LE12 9NH. Tel: 01509 500 300. E-mail: info@sip-group.com. Website: www.sip-group.com. High quality DIY/professional welding equipment, portable generators, and air tools.

Thatcham (The Motor Insurance Repair Research Centre) Colthrop Lane, Thatcham, Newbury, Berks, RG19 4NR. E-mail: enquiries@thatcham.org. Website: www.thatcham.org. The insurance industry testing body. The fitting of an approved device helps safeguard your Discovery and can lead to worthwhile insurance discounts.

VSIB (Vehicle Security Installation Board) Bates Business Centre, Church Road, Harold Wood, Romford, Essex, RM3 0JF. Tel: 01708 340911. The governing body of top-quality security installers.

Wakefields Stanford Hall, Ashby Road, Stanford-on-Soar LE12 5QW. Tel: 01509 857 200. Website: www.wakefields.co.uk. Distributors of workshop storage equipment.

The Walnut Dash Company Prestige House, 92 Hythe Hill, Colchester, Essex, CO1 2NH. Tel: 01206 791888. E-mail: info@walnutdash.com. Website: www.walnutdashcompany.com. Suppliers of high quality, self-adhesive precision-cut walnut trim for all Discovery models, complete with a ten-year warranty. Also repairs of existing wooden trim.

SPECIALIST MAGAZINES

Land Rover Enthusiast PO Box 178, Wallingford DO, Oxfordshire, OX10 8PD. Tel: 01491 201488. E-mail: j.taylor@landroverenthusiast.com. Website: www.landroverenthusiast.com.

Land Rover Monthly The Golden Gate Production Co. Ltd, 2 Brickfields Business Park, Woolpit, Suffolk, IP30 9QS. Tel: 01359 240066. E-mail: editorial@lrm.co.uk. Website: www.lrm.co.uk.

Land Rover Owner EMAP Automotive Ltd., Media House, Lynchwood, Peterborough Business Park, Peterborough, Cambs, PE2 6EA. Tel: 01733 468582. E-mail: landroverowner@bauermedia.co.uk. Website: www.lro.com.

Land Rover World IPC Focus Network, Leon House, 233 High Street, Croydon, CR9 1HZ. Tel: 0208 726 8000. Website: www.landroverworld.co.uk. Email: landroverworld@ipcmedia.com.

CLUBS AND ORGANISATIONS

Camel Trophy Owners Club
E-mail: secretary@cameltrophy.org
Website: www.cameltrophy.org

Discovery Owners Club
E-mail: memsec@discoveryownersclub.org
Website: www.discoveryownersclub.org

G4 Owners Club
Email: secretary@g4ownersclub.com
Website: www.g4ownersclub.com

Specifications and production figures

Discovery Series 1

ENGINES

Petrol	Capacity (cc)	Bore x stroke (mm)	Power bhp @ rpm	Torque lb ft @ rpm	Compression ratio	Main gearbox	Auto option	Transfer gearbox
V8 (carburettor)	3,528	88.9x71.1	144.5 @ 5,000	192 @ 2,000	8.13:1	LT77	N/A	LT230T
V8 Fuel injection	3,528	88.9x71.1	163 @ 4,750	212 @ 3,000	9.35:1	LT77 (S)	ZF 4HP22	LT230T
			153 @ 4,750	192 @ 3,000	8.13:1 (cat)			
V8 Fuel injection >1994	3,947	94.0x71.1	180 @ 4,750	230 @ 3,100	9.35:1 (cat)	LT77S	ZF 4HP22	LT230T
V8 Fuel injection 1994 on	3,947	94.0x71.1	180 @ 4,750	230 @ 3,100	9.35:1 (cat)	R380	ZF 4HP22	LT230T
Mpi four-cylinder > 1994	1,994	84.5x89.0	134 @ 6,000	137 @ 2,500	10.0:1	LT77S	N/A	LT230T
Mpi four-cylinder 1994 on	1,994	84.5x89.0	134 @ 6,000	140 @ 3,600	10.0:1	R380	N/A	LT230T

Diesel	Capacity (cc)	Bore x stroke (mm)	Power bhp @ rpm	Torque lb ft @ rpm	Compression ratio	Main gearbox	Auto option	Transfer gearbox
200 Tdi	2,495	90.47x97.0	111 @ 4,000	195 @ 1,800	19.5:1	LT77 (S)	ZF 4HP22	LT230T
300 Tdi	2,495	90.47x97.0	111 @ 4,000	195 @ 1,800	19.5:1	R380	ZF 4HP22	LT230T
300 Tdi (auto only)	2,495	90.47x97.0	120 @ 4,000	221 @ 1,800	19.5:1	R380	ZF 4HP22	LT230T

GENERAL NOTES

The automatic gearbox option was phased in throughout the life cycle of the Series 1 Discovery and was not necessarily available on all years of all models.

The LT77 gearbox was slightly uprated in 1991 and became the LT77S as a result.

The 300 Tdi was given a slight power and torque boost in 1996 but only when used in conjunction with the automatic gearbox, in order to improve acceleration and in-gear performance.

VITAL STATISTICS

	200 Tdi	300 Tdi	V8	MPi
Wheelbase (mm)	2,540	2,540	2,540	2,540
Track front & rear (mm)	1,486	1,486	1,486	1,486
Overall length (mm)	4,521	4,484	4,521	4,521
Overall width (mm)	1,793	2,189	1,793	1,793
Overall height (mm)	1,928	1,914	1,928	1,918
EEC kerb weight (kg)**	2,008 3-door	2,040 3-door	1,979	1,890 3-door
	2,053 5-door	2,065 5-door		1,925 5-door
Max gross vehicle weight (kg)	2,720	2,720	2,720	2,720
Max trailer towing weight (kg)	750 unbraked	750 unbraked	750 unbraked	750 unbraked
	3,500 over-run brakes	3,500 over-run brakes	3,500 over-run brakes	2,750 over-run brakes

** All models: EEC kerb weight is defined as the unladen weight plus a full tank of fuel plus a driver weighing 75kg.

STEERING

All models featured power-assisted steering of the worm and roller type, produced by Adwest. Lock-to-lock requires 3.375 turns.

SUSPENSION

Coil springs are fitted at each corner, single rate at the front, dual rate at the rear, together with conventional hydraulic dampers. The front beam axle is located by radius arms (running front to rear) and a Panhard rod transversely. At the rear, the beam axle is located by trailing links and a central 'A' frame.

Discovery Series 2

ENGINES

Petrol	Capacity (cc)	Bore x stroke (mm)	Power bhp @ rpm	Torque lb ft @ rpm	Compression ratio	Main gearbox	Auto option	Transfer gearbox
V8	3,947	–	182.4 @ 4,750	250.8 @ 2,600	9.35:1	R380	ZF 4HP22 EH	LT230Q

Diesel	Capacity (cc)	Bore x stroke (mm)	Power bhp @ rpm	Torque lb ft @ rpm	Compression ratio	Main gearbox	Auto option	Transfer gearbox
Td5	2,495	–	136 @ 4,200	221 @ 1,950	–	R380	–	LT230Q
Td5	2,495	–	136 @ 4,200	232 @ 1,950	–	ZF 4HP22 HE (auto)	–	LT230Q

VITAL STATISTICS

	Td5	V8
Wheelbase (mm)	2,540	2,540
Track front & rear (mm)	1,540/1,560	1,540/1,560
Overall length (mm)	4,705	4,705
Overall width (mm)	1,793	1,793
Overall height (mm)	1,940	1,940
EEC kerb weight (kg)**	2,205	2,020
Max gross vehicle weight (kg)	2,720	2,720
Max trailer towing weight (kg)	750 unbraked	750 unbraked
	3,500 over-run brakes	3,500 over-run brakes

Discovery 2003

ENGINES

Petrol	Capacity (cc)	Bore x stroke (mm)	Power bhp @ rpm	Torque lb ft @ rpm	Compression ratio	Main gearbox	Auto option	Transfer gearbox
V8	3,950	–	185 @ 4,750	250 @ 2,600	9.35:1	R380	ZF 4HP22 EH	LT230Q

Diesel	Capacity (cc)	Bore x stroke (mm)	Power bhp @ rpm	Torque lb ft @ rpm	Compression ratio	Main gearbox	Auto option	Transfer gearbox
Td5	2,495	–	137 @ 4,200	220 @ 1,950	19.5:1	R380	–	LT230Q
Td5	2,495	–	137 @ 4,200	250 @ 1,950	19.5:1	ZF 4HP22 HE (auto)	–	LT230Q

VITAL STATISTICS

	Td5	V8
Wheelbase (mm)	2,540	2,540
Track front & rear (mm)	1,540/1,560	1,540/1,560
Overall length (mm)	4,705	4,705
Overall width (mm)	1,885	1,885
Overall height (mm)	1,900 (1,940 with roof bars)	1,900 (1,940 with roof bars)
EEC kerb weight (kg)**	2,175–2,270	2,175–2,270
Max gross vehicle weight (kg)	2,825	2,825
	(air & HD coil suspension)	(air & HD coil suspension)
Max trailer towing weight (kg)	750 unbraked	750 unbraked
	3,500 over-run brakes	3,500 over-run brakes

Discovery Series 3

ENGINE	V6 Diesel	V6 Petrol	V8 Petrol
Layout	Longitudinal	Longitudinal	Longitudinal
No. cylinders/valves	V6/24	V6/24	V8/32
Effective displacement	2720cc	4009cc	4394cc
Bore/stroke	81/88mm	100.4/84.4mm	88/90.3mm
Compression ratio	17.3:1	9.75:1	10.5:1
Max. power @ rpm	140kW @ 4000	160kW @ 4500	220kW @ 5500
Max. torque @ rpm	440Nm @ 1900	360Nm @ 3000	425Nm @ 4000
PERFORMANCE			
Max speed	112mph/180kph	112mph/180kph	121mph/195kph
0-60mph – auto (manual)	11.7sec (11.2sec)	10.6sec	8.0sec
0-100kph	12.8sec (11.5sec)	10.9sec	8.6sec

VITAL STATISTICS

No. of seats	5/7 option	5/7 option	5/7 option
LENGTH			
Overall	4835mm	4835mm	4835mm
Wheelbase	2885mm	2885mm	2885mm
WIDTH			
Excluding/including mirrors	1915/2190mm	1915/2190mm	1915/2190mm
With mirrors folded	2009mm	2009mm	2009mm
HEIGHT			
Fixed roof	1887mm	1887mm	1887mm
Glass roof	1882mm	1882mm	1882mm
With sunroof open	1920mm	1920mm	1920mm
With roof side rails	1891mm	1891mm	1891mm
With roof antennae module	1940mm	1940mm	1940mm
INTERIOR			
Leg room in row two	955mm	955mm	955mm
Head room in row two, fixed roof	1043mm	1043mm	1043mm
Head room in row two, glass roof	1076 mm	1076 mm	1076 mm
Front shoulder room	1503mm	1503mm	1503mm
Rear shoulder room in row two	1508mm	1508mm	1508mm

EXTERIOR

Max ground clearance (air suspension)	240mm	240mm	240mm
Track – front/rear	1605/1612.5mm	1605/1612.5mm	1605/1612.5mm
Suspension articulation – front/rear	255/330mm	255/330mm	255/330mm
Wading depth (max)	700mm	700mm	700mm
Turning circle – kerb-to-kerb	11.45m	11.45m	11.45m
Turning circle – lock-to-lock	3.3 turns	3.3 turns	3.3 turns
Drag coefficient	0.41Cd	0.41Cd	0.41Cd
Max loadspace volume	2558l	2558l	2558l
Approach angle (max)	37.2°	37.2°	37.2°
Departure angle (max)	29.6°	29.6°	29.6°
Departure angle with spare tyre (max)	28.1°	28.1°	28.1°
Departure angle with towbar (max)	18.5°	18.5°	18.5°
Max laden weight	3230kg	3230kg	3230kg
Max towing weight (braked trailer)	3500kg	3500kg	3500kg
Max towing weight (unbraked trailer)	750kg	750kg	750kg

OVERALL GEARING

Transfer box ratio (high/low)	1:1/2.93:1	1:1/2.93:1	1:1/2.93:1

Manual:

1st (high/low)	15.596:1/45.694:1	N/A	N/A
2nd (high/low)	8.608:1/25.223:1	N/A	N/A
3rd (high/low)	5.474:1/16.038:1	N/A	N/A
4th (high/low)	3.868:1/11.334:1	N/A	N/A
5th (high/low)	3.070:1/8.995:1	N/A	N/A
6th (high/low)	2.563:1/7.509:1	N/A	N/A
Reverse (high/low)	14.506:1/42.501:1	N/A	N/A

Auto

1st (high/low)	14.765:1/43.259:1	15.558:1/45.581:1	15.558:1/45.581:1
2nd (high/low)	8.284:1/24.284:1	8.723:1/25.588:1	8.723:1/25.588:1
3rd (high/low)	5.384:1/15.788:1	5.673:1/16.636:1	5.673:1/16.636:1
4th (high/low)	4.046:1/11.859:1	4.263:1/12.496:1	4.263:1/12.496:1
5th (high/low)	3.069:1/8.992:1	3.234:1/9.474:1	3.234:1/9.474:1
6th (high/low)	2.446:1/7.151:1	2.557:1/7.535:1	2.557:1/7.535:1
Reverse (high/low)	12.047:1/35.258:1	12.693:1/37.151:1	12.693:1/37.151:1

FUEL

Fuel tank capacity	82.3 litres	86.3 litres	86.3 litres

DRIVE SYSTEM
Full-time four-wheel-drive with electronically-controlled centre differential and optional electronically-controlled rear differential.

PRODUCTION TOTALS

Getting exact figures for Discovery production is notoriously difficult, but regardless, the Discovery has been a startlingly popular vehicle, a measure of which can be seen from the fact that in 12 years it breached the half-million mark. Moreover, this total beats the Range Rover by almost 40,000 units, despite having less than half the number of years to do so.

Year	Total	Year	Total	Year	Total
1989	3,748	1996	65,034	2003	46,165
1990	23,050	1997	58,351	2004	42,339
1991	19,260	1998	49,785	(combined S2/S3)	
1992	24,340	1999	54,800	2005	56,206
1993	35,625	2000	56,360	2006	50,633
1994	54,424	2001	41,549	2007	44,538
1995	69,998	2002	45,918	**Total**	**842,123**

Numerology

VIN: Vehicle Identification Number

On Series 1 Discoverys the VIN can be found stamped on an aluminium plate which is riveted to the slam panel, alongside the bonnet lock. It comprises a minimum of 17 characters containing a complex code, which can reveal much about the car in question. A typical number might read thus: SAL LJ G M M 3 N A 000000. These characters denote:

SAL   'SA' denotes Rover, and 'L' Land Rover.

LJ   The model reference for the Discovery; all models will have this.

G   The basic model code; almost all models will show a 'G' at this point, the only variation being 'D' for a Honda Crossroad.

M   The body type code, being 'B' for a three-door and 'M' for a five-door.

M   The engine code, being 'V' for 3.5-litre carburetted V8, 'L' for 3.5-litre EFi V8, 'M' for 3.9-litre EFi V8, 'Y' for 2-litre four-cylinder petrol, and 'F' for all Tdi engines.

3   The code denoting which gearbox is fitted and the side of the steering wheel, thus: '7' for right-hand drive manual, '3' for right-hand drive auto, '8' for left-hand drive manual, and '4' for left-hand drive auto.

N   The year of manufacture, thus: 'G' 1990, 'H' 1991, 'J' 1992, 'K' 1993, 'L' 1994, 'M' 1995, 'N' 1996, 'P' 1997, 'R' 1998, and 'S' 1999.

A   A simple reference for the place of assembly in this case, Solihull.

000000 The actual serial number of the vehicle, in this case clearly not possible, but included for the sake of illustration.

By getting to grips with this number you can use it as part of your pre-buying check; it is not uncommon for vehicles which left the factory with a V8 engine to have been converted at some point to diesel power. The VIN will confirm this, and in such a case would alert you to ensure that all the relevant aspects of the conversion have been carried out correctly. Moreover, your insurers will also need to be informed – more importantly, if you have an accident where your insurers inspect the vehicle and find a conversion, it could be used as a lever to avoid paying out.

Series 2 cars had a different code set-up to Series 1 models (see below).

↑ **VIN numbers are increasingly important in the fight against car crime.**

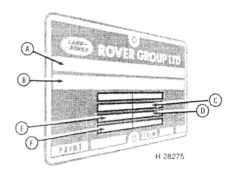

↑ **This diagram shows the general layout of the plate. The meanings of the various references are: A – Type approval reference; B – VIN number (this must be a minimum of 17 characters); C – Maximum permitted weight of vehicle (kg); D – Maximum permitted vehicle and trailer weight (kg); E – Maximum road weight, front axle (kg); and F – Maximum road weight, rear axle (kg).**

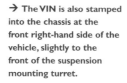
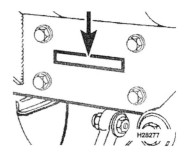

→ **The VIN is also stamped into the chassis at the front right-hand side of the vehicle, slightly to the front of the suspension mounting turret.**

Engine Numbers

All engine numbers should match that shown on the V5. The engine may well have been changed at some point, but that's no reason for a mismatch, as a legitimate change should have been notified as a matter of course to the DVLA.

Series 2

The Series 2 cars were launched in the 1999 model year, and though the VIN plates were more or less in the same position the VIN codes changed slightly, as shown in the table below.
Our example code is; SAL LT G M 2 3 2 A 000000.

SAL   This denotes the world-wide manufacturer code. In this case, 'SA' represents the Rover Group and 'L' denotes that it has been produced by Land Rover as part of the overall company.

LT   The model code for the Series 2, changed from the LJ code of Series 1 cars.

G   Again this makes a specific reference to the Japanese market, which is denoted as 'A', with all other models being 'G'.

M   This is the body style, being a choice that's no choice as the Series 2 car comes only in five-door format.

2   This is the engine code: '1' stands for V8 in Australia only, '2' for V8 in EEC countries and Japan, '3' for V8 in all other countries, '7' for Td5 world-wide with the exception of '9' for Td5 in EEC countries, Australia, and Japan.

3   The code denoting which gearbox is fitted and the side of the steering wheel, thus: '7' is right-hand drive manual, '3' is right-hand drive auto, '8' is left-hand drive manual, and '4' is left-hand drive auto.

2   The year of manufacture, thus: 'X' is 1999, 'Y' is 2000, '1' is 2001, '2' is 2002, etc.

A   A simple reference for the place of assembly in this case, Solihull.

000000 The actual serial number of the vehicle, in this case clearly not possible, but included for the sake of illustration.

↑ The engine number on Tdi engines is stamped on the cylinder block on the right-hand side of the engine, above the camshaft front cover plate.

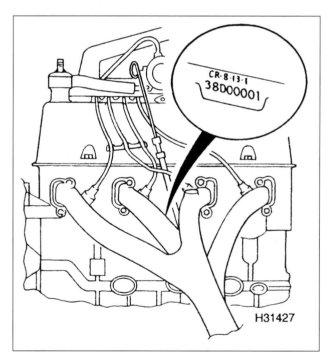

↑ V8 engines are stamped on the cylinder block, between cylinders three and five (left-hand side of the engine – as shown here).
The Mpi number is stamped on the right-hand face of the cylinder block, alongside the gearbox.

Technical information

Car manufacturers and aftermarket suppliers regularly mix and match terminology, which combines with the UK's gradual conversion from imperial to metric to make it increasingly tricky for the Discovery owner to get a total grip on what's what.

This simple conversion table will help to ensure that you get it right every time.

	To	Multiply by
Length		
Inches	Millimetres	25.4
Millimetres	Inches	0.0394
Miles	Kilometres	1.609
Kilometres	Miles	0.621
Volume		
Cubic inches	Cubic centimetres	16.387
Cubic centimetres	Cubic inches	0.061
Imperial gallons	Litres	4.546
Litres	Imperial gallons	0.22
Weight		
Pounds	Kilograms	0.454
Kilograms	Pounds	2.205
Speed		
Mph	Kph	1.609
Kph	Mph	0.621
Fuel consumption		
Imperial mpg	Kilometres per litre	0.354
Kilometres per litre	Imperial mpg	2.825

Bolt identification: metric/imperial and thread sizes

When it comes to sorting out bolt identification, look for an 'S' or an 'R' stamped into the head, which denotes that it is imperial. The threads on imperial fasteners are shown as threads per inch (TPI).

Imperial Threads Per Inch (TPI)

	4BA	2BA	No.10	1/4"	5/16"	3/8"	7/16"
BA	38.5	31.4	–	–	–	–	–
UNC	–	–	24	20	18	16	14
UNF	–	–	32	28	24	24	20
BSF	–	–	–	26	22	20	18
BSW	–	–	–	20	18	16	14

The figure '8.8' in the head shows that it is a metric bolt. On metric bolts, the pitch is the length of ten threads, so a bolt described as M10 x 1.5 pitch is one with a shank diameter of 10mm where ten threads cover a distance of 1.5cm. The table below shows the pitches used on most metric bolts (the exception being the pitch on Japanese 10mm bolts, which for some reason is a finer 1.25 rather than the usual 1.5).

Bolt size	Pitch (mm)
M5	0.8
M6	1.00
M8	1.25
M10	1.5
M12	1.75

Index

Page numbers in *italics* refer to illustration captions.